FILM PRODUCING

LOW-BUDGET FILMS
THAT SELL

FILM
PRODUCING
LOW-BUDGET
FILMS
that SELL

by
RENEE HARMON

SAMUEL FRENCH
HOLLYWOOD

Copyright © 1988 by Renee Harmon

First Samuel French edition

Library of Congress Cataloging-in-Publication Data
Harmon, Renee
[Complete guide to low budget film production]
Film producing: low budget films that sell / by Renee Harmon.
p. cm.
Reprint. Originally published: Complete guide to low budget film production.
Dubuque, Iowa: Kendall/Hunt, c1985.
1. Motion Pictures--Finance.
2. Motion pictures--Production and direction. I. Title
PN1993.5.A1H2B 1989   791.43'0232--dc19   89-80343
ISBN 0-573-60699-4

Cover design by Tony Gleeson
Printed on acid free paper
Printed and bound in the United States of America

Published and distributed by
Samuel French Trade
7623 Sunset Boulevard
Hollywood, CA 90046

Fade in . . .

Fade in...

This book has been written for you—the writer, director, actor or cinematographer who wants to try his hand at producing a motion picture. Every single one of you is an expert in your own field. Many times over you have demonstrated your technical knowledge and your artistic ability. The time has come for you to get control over the decisions affecting your creative work. You want to be the one who stays on top of your project from beginning to end—

You want to be a PRODUCER.

The term producer is amorphous. It covers such a broad spectrum of people and responsibilities. The producer's position itself has changed drastically over the past years. During the heyday of the old studio system, a producer was only an administrator who supervised an assigned project—he had little artistic control. The position of the producer did not emerge as a filmmaking force until the anti-trust ruling broke the theaters away from the studios. Still, the independent producer only gained some measure of influence once the major studios steered away from production and put more emphasis on distribution deals.

Today, all kinds of independent producers are making films. There are the ones who have mega-dollars at their disposal, others to whom a budget of three to four million dollars represents a "low-budget film," and still others who speak about "top dollars" once their budget hits the $300,000 mark.

This book is addressed to you, the small, *low-budget* film producer who faces the gargantuan task of bringing in a motion picture between $100,000 and $300,000. Over the last few years, the small, low-budget film producer has gained in importance. Looking at the rapidly expanding fields of home video and cable (domestically, as well as overseas) it doesn't take a crystal ball to realize his increasing importance. His films are now being exhibited at *all* the important film markets such as Cannes (France), Milan (Italy), Manila (Philippines) and the American Film Market (Los Angeles).

The low-budget film has proven itself right next to its top dollar competitors. Contrary to common belief, the average buyer doesn't care about the cost of a film (blockbusters excepted), but is only interested in the film itself. That is to say, he considers the professional look of the film, the story line, and most importantly, the intangible *something* that transmits excitement from the screen to the viewer.

1

Yes, there is definitely a place for the small, low-budget film producer in the high-powered field of motion picture production. A major stumbling block for many novice producers—"the new kids on the block"—has been their own vision and understanding of the producer's position. Most producers who are starting out on their first venture have potentially successful and creative ideas, yet for the simple fact that they approach their goal in an inappropriate way, only a handful will realize their dreams.

It is a fallacy to believe that the small independent producer needs *money* and *connections* to get his first film on the screen. I had neither when I started my film producing company six years ago, and at the time of this writing CIARA PRODUCTIONS, INC. has four feature films in domestic and overseas release. When I started out, I had nothing but a goal, and training and experience in the areas of writing and acting.

Believe me, if you are an expert in *any* of the fields relating to motion pictures (writing, acting, directing, cinematography) you are ready to start your own production company. Yet, by the same token, you must be humble enough to realize that you know about *one area only*, and therefore are willing to learn about the rest.

All too often, the beginning producer is hesitant to acknowledge the borders of his expertise, and extends his control into areas he should leave alone.

FILM PRODUCING: LOW-BUDGET FILMS THAT SELL aims to provide you with all the needed information about:

Financing
Screenplay Writing
Directing
Acting
Casting
Editing
Crew Requirements
Equipment Requirements
Legal Aspects and Insurance
Distribution and Advertising

This book will take you through *all* the phases of *producing a 'selling film.'* Many of the questions and problems that may arise will be answered and discussed. But most importantly, FILM PRODUCING offers easy-to-follow guidelines, as it identifies the structural and stylistic elements of the effective motion picture, and presents step by step comprehensive techniques to produce a professional picture.

So, let's roll up our sleeves, and set the slate for SCENE I—TAKE I

Chapter One
Financing

It is true that the independent film producer needs imagination to find the necessary financing for his film, but the low-budget filmmaker needs an additional portion of courage and ingenuity to surmount the obstacles in his way. The odds of getting his film financed are indeed very small. The risk of investment in motion pictures has risen steadily since the advent of television. It is a sad truth, but the odds against a picture playing in its negative cost* have risen sharply, while the odds of "hitting the jackpot" have dwindled considerably. Many pictures are ending in the red. Making a picture, no matter how small or large the budget, is always a risk. One needs only to remember that the production and distribution arms of feature films have been fighting a losing battle for the past twenty years. One wonders why this industry survives, and finds the answer in the obsession of the filmmakers, and the fact that many major studios have been absorbed by conglomerates that use the filmmaking segment of their industries to absorb the gains made by more profitable segments of their vast holdings. Looking at the independent film producer, focusing primarily upon the low-budget filmmaker, we have to face the fact that only ten percent of all their productions will find a distributor. Out of this ten percent, only a few will make a marginal profit.

Looking at filmmaking in this light, you would probably refuse to put your hard-earned dollars on such a chancy investment. Still, you, the new low-budget film producer, are determined to get your film off the ground. If nothing can keep you from making your dream come true, good for you. Maybe you will see your film on the screen, maybe it will play in at least its negative cost, and maybe—just maybe—your investors will earn a small profit.

Before we delve any further into the murky waters of film financing, it might be a good idea to take a look at your respective strengths and weaknesses. Before raising any money, you must know where you stand. So, let's first take a survey of your weaknesses:

1. You may lack a track record. You may have only one, or possibly no feature film at all to your credit. In this case, you should make a strong effort to interest in your project a director known for his reliability. This man should have a number of films to his credit. He

---

*"Negative cost" refers to the actual amount of money needed to produce the picture.

should be a director known to "bring the picture in on time *and* on budget." If you have the choice between the creative and the reliable director, by all means choose the reliable one.

2. One of the most common and hardest hurdles to overcome is the fact that your own track record might be slim, or worse, "zilch." In any case, you are in foreign and still uncharted territory. You might have a sensitive art picture to your credit, or some industrials or documentaries. It doesn't matter, you'll have to prove yourself all over again. My advice is to soothe the investors' qualms with a completion bond. A completion bond is a form of insurance. The bonding company will step in in case the film goes over budget, or is in danger of not being completed.

3. You probably will be unable to attract a distributor to your planned project. Most likely, any distributor of standing wants to see at least the rough cut* of your film before committing himself. If you are fortunate, and if your film shows promise, then you might get a "letter of intent." In such a letter, the distribution company states its "intent" of representing your picture. (You see, there is a fine line. They will not "guarantee" the distribution of your film.) They most likely will state how your picture will fill their needs, will outline some distribution plans and a tentative release date. I agree, such a letter of intent looks terrific. In some cases it will even calm the jittery nerves of a prospective investor, at least long enough for him to sign a check. Still, anyone with some knowledge of the film business is aware of the vaporous legal consistency of such a document. The intent letter doesn't hold the distribution company to anything. The small print states that the distributor will only represent your film if it meets his "technical requirements." As anyone knows, any technical fault can be found easily in even the best film. Yet, the agreement will hold *you*, the producer, in iron fists. If the distributor likes the film, it is his and his alone. In reality, such an agreement will keep you from signing with another company that offers more favorable terms.

4. Since the budget for your film will be relatively small, you will have difficulties raising money. Strange as it sounds, most investors are very leery about investing in any low-budget film. They feel much more secure and comfortable parting with sizable chunks of their dough.

But don't despair. You, the low-budget filmmaker, will show considerable areas of strength. Use this strength wisely as you sit down at the bargaining table.

---

*In the latter stages of editing, prior to the fine cut, the rough cut will give some idea of the finished product. At this point, dialog has been added, but neither music nor sound effects have been mixed in.

4

1. You will be able to bring in a picture of a quality close to the one your friend produces for ten times the amount you require. Your picture is not burdened with studio overhead. These are expenditures which will increase the budget considerably, without adding anything to the production value.

2. The break even point on your picture is much lower than on a picture costing several millions. Your picture, if correctly released and exhibited, will be out of the red sooner than the more costly one.

3. Your picture will have a fairly long life. As your picture "bicycles" through the country, it may have a life span of at least three years.

Keeping in mind the fact that most of the independently produced films fall into the 2-4 million range, we will first look at the usual forms of financing available for such projects. Understanding this type of financing is still light years away from your own financial requirements. Your small, low-budget film belongs in a different ball park. Still, let's shed some light on these "Olympian" patterns of getting "the dough." One never knows, you might move within this exalted sphere sooner than you think.

Financing is considered to be twofold—*Development Financing* and *Production Financing*.

Development Financing

Development financing, also at times called "seed money," covers the (often high) costs for optioning the screenplay, the director and principal cast, including—as everyone prays—a "bankable" star. It also covers budgeting and legal costs, as well as all monies spent on "raising money." Finding development financing is probably the most arduous task. Imagine, you are asking people to invest in a *non-existing* commodity that may never materialize.

Production Financing

Production financing will refund all development financing. It will also pay for the pre-production, production and post-production of your movie. Production financing can be raised the following ways:

Negative Pickup
TV and Cable Pre-sale
Co-production
Venture Capital
Limited Partnerships
Foreign Investment

Negative Pickup

In a *negative pickup,* the rights of a motion picture (theatrical, TV, cable or home video) are being licensed to a distributor or several distributors for an advance. The concept is that the distributor will pay the producer a stated sum of money upon delivery of the picture. Usually, in addition, the distributor has to pay a small amount of money at the start of principal photography. This sum is an advance against a percentage of the income of the film. Whether this amount is to be paid from the gross or net receipts of the motion picture is open to negotiation. In any case, at the completion of the film, the producer can expect a sum less than the production cost. At times, producers use the advance sum as collateral for a bank loan. However, as soon as he receives a bank loan, the producer must provide a completion bond.

The distributor agreeing to a *negative pickup* usually decides to have some loopholes in the contract. The picture might turn out truly horrible, or the theme might not be up-to-date any more, or . . . we could go on and on. In any case, be aware of loopholes. A contract containing loopholes cannot be used for obtaining a bank loan. For this reason it is important that the contract lists exactly the elements that the producer must deliver. Usually, the producer agrees to deliver a film based upon a screenplay that the distributor has approved. The producer should be very careful about changing the script. If the finished film deviates considerably from the approved script, the distributor has grounds to cancel the agreement. Often, the distribution company wants to approve the budget to make certain that a specified amount of money will be expended. Also, the producer most likely has to agree to certain standards as far as the technical quality of the motion picture is concerned. Yet, he should scream and kick if the distributor requests certain artistic qualities. These elements are too intangible and too open to subjective interpretation.

If you are in the fortunate position that one of the majors (Universal, Warners, 20th-Century Fox, Columbia) has signed a negative pickup with you, you will be given a "letter of credit" (LC). This LC spells out, loud and clear, that the respective studio is backing your project with its own credit resources. In this case, a bank will be interested in granting a loan for your project. You even might be able to borrow the entire required amount from the bank.

In order to appreciate the bank's position regarding motion picture loans, we must remember that motion pictures are *not* bankable risks. No bank will grant any loan for anything if the only source of repayment depends upon monies earned by the project. In this respect, the credit available from the bank depends on the risk standing of the risk taker. Assuming that the LC came from a smaller company of less risk standing than one of the majors, then the risk taker has to pledge assets such as real estate or his interest in other pictures as collateral.

Once a loan has been granted, you will be able to borrow funds on a "floating budget"—that is to say, as needed during the time of pre-production, production and post-production. These advances will usually be made weekly, and each request must be verified by the appropriate reports listing each budget item. The interest rate that you'll have to pay will be slightly above the prime lending rate, and most banks expect to have the loan repaid twenty-two months after the release date. This clause may prove to be a serious headache for the producer, if for any reason either production or release date has to be postponed. The documents that you'll have to furnish are numerous. In your darker moments you'll compare their girth with that of "War and Peace" on your bookshelf. Following is a list of the most important papers that the bank will require:

1. Chain of title proving the ownership of the literary property upon which the motion picture is based. Remember, this is a very important document—the person or persons owning the literary property do own the motion picture.
2. Budget (of course).
3. Letter of credit, or financial statement, and guarantee of collateral of the risk takers.
4. Distribution agreement providing for recoupment of the production monies expended.

Once these documents have been furnished, the bank will happily draw up its own papers:

1. A security agreement. This is a first lien on the literary property upon which the motion picture is based, a first lien on the picture itself, and another first lien on the producer's share of profits (you see, they do not take any chances).
2. Distributor's agreement:
   (a) The distributor agrees to pay the producer's share of receipts to the bank (in case you, the producer, have any visions of skipping the country).
   (b) The distributor agrees to limit print and advertising expenses to some agreed upon amount.
3. Agreements with anyone holding rights to the picture, stating that these rights will be secondary to the bank's right.
4. Laboratory pledgeholders agreement.
5. Loan agreement between the bank and the production company stating the terms of the loan.

TV and Cable Pre-sale

These deals work similarly to the negative pickup. Yet, there is one difference. Most likely, the producer will *not* receive any actual cash upon delivery of his picture. But the network's* letter of agreement is *bankable*, that is to say, it can be used as collateral if the producer supplies a completion bond. But beware, only the network's letters of agreement are bankable. Any such letter from a TV or cable distribution company supplying syndicated stations with product cannot be used as collateral for a bank loan.

Venture Capital

There are some investment firms which provide high risk capital for various business ventures. Your broker, attorney or CPA might know about such firms, and might be able to steer you in the right direction. Still, most of these firms are not highly receptive to the small, low-budget producer. Even if you have a proven track record, they will be hesitant to deal with you.

Co-productions

Some independent producers are willing to work together. You should be highly selective about the co-producing company you choose. The agreement should be drawn up by an attorney knowledgeable in the motion picture field. I would like to discourage any new producer from such a venture. Entering a co-production with another company carries the risk that you, the less experienced one, may lose control over your project. Possibly, you might also lose money. Unless you own a terrific, sure-fire script, any established and reliable production company will be more than hesitant to join forces with a novice producer.

Foreign Investment

During the past years, foreign financing has become important for the American producer. Of course, to warrant foreign interest, the budget of the proposed motion picture must be significant, the stars under consideration must be known world wide, and most importantly, the story itself must have international interest. It is interesting to observe that, ". . . with the exception of the United States almost every film producing country of the world subsidizes the production of motion pictures within its border...." **

About twenty film producing nations offer subsidies to the independent American production company. It is not out of the goodness of their hearts that they offer us money, but simply to protect their own motion picture industry. For this reason it is obvious that the American producer desiring to shoot a film under their sponsorship must agree to their demands. Most foreign regulations provide for the following:

1. The American production company must agree to shoot the feature film within the borders of said country.
2. Only local laboratories will be used to develop and print the film, and to provide the sound work.
3. Only local crews will be used.
4. The American production company is permitted to employ only two American "key elements"—that is to say, they may either bring two American stars, or one American star and one American director on the project. The script has to be approved by the host country to ensure the story is not detrimental to its image.
5. All supplies have to be purchased in the host country.

*ABC, NBC, CBS are networks in contrast to the privately owned TV stations, also called syndicated stations.
**Journal of the Producers Guild of America, September, 1968.

After we've learned about the requirements and regulations involving foreign shoots, let's take another look at the sources of money available to the American producer.

1. Cash subsidies
2. Low interest or no interest government loans
3. Advances of partial production cost
4. Foreign tax shelters

Cash Subsidies

Canada, Australia, Greece and at times Yugoslavia provide direct loans for motion pictures ensuring a substantial "national content." That is to say, the film must be shot in the respective country, with their cast and crew, using the post-production facilities available within their borders. To receive such cash subsidies the American producer should join forces with a production company from the respective country. Your best bet is to contact the consulate of the country where you wish to produce your film, asking them to get you in touch with their Film Commission. This agency will be able to furnish you with names of reliable production companies.

Low Interest Or No Interest Government Loans

Great Britain, France, Italy and Germany provide these loans. However, a substantial portion of the "loans" come in the form of "studio investment." That is to say, contributing many of the below-the-line costs of the project.* It is not easy to obtain such a loan. Countries interested in granting government loans will strongly consider all legal entities of the production. Of secondary importance are cast, director and locations.

Foreign Tax Shelters

Canada and Germany offer tax shelters. The basic concept of such a tax shelter deal sounds simple, even though it is highly complicated. Let's say that the foreign investor interested in "sheltering" some of his money will invest a million dollars in your project. He then has to prove that the "actual" value of the shelter (your film) will be about three million on the open market. In other words, he expects that your film will "play in" three million. Then he can base his shelter on the estimated market value. Tax shelter deals should not be entered unless you know your way around. Secondly, you should never attempt to consider such a deal unless you are assisted by an attorney who is knowledgeable in the tax laws of the respective country. A well-versed attorney who is skilled in the packaging of domestic deals will most likely be able to direct you to these foreign tax shelters. Again, your budget has to be in the several million range to qualify.

*Below-the-line cost refers to the mechanics of production such as studio rental, cost of developing and printing film, sound work, etc.

Advances Of Partial Production Cost

Austria and West Berlin are your most likely sources for this type of financing. Here again, the foreign investment does not come in either cash or loans, but in the respective country's participation in the below-the-line cost. Austria as well as West Berlin will provide locations, studio facilities, crews, and post-production facilities, as well as services. To qualify for such a partnership, the American producer must supply fifty percent of the actual budget.

Financing for the Low-Budget Producer

It does not take a crystal ball to see that the types of financing we have discussed on the previous pages are pretty well in the realm of wishful thinking for the low-budget film producer. The yet "unproven" but hard working and enthusiastic filmmaker is limited to two forms of financing:

1. Limited partnership
2. Elbow grease financing

Limited Partnership

In a limited partnership, the investors become limited partners and acquire non-transferable partnership interest. The limited partner is protected from liability in excess of his investment. You should remember that the standard limited partnership agreement provides that the limited partners (your investors) receive 50% of the net profits, and the general partner (the producer) receives 50% of the net profits. However, the producer will not share in any profits until the total investment of the limited partners has been repaid to them. The limited partnership agreement usually provides a fee for the producer, and the reimbursement of any expenses he incurs in connection with the production of the film.

The latter clause has at times proven to be a "red herring." Every so often, unreliable producers have taken advantage of this clause. They brought together a group of limited partners whose total investment was far too slim to justify any production. Usually the scheme went as such: The producer showed an interesting script and got a group of investors together. After he had drawn sizable amounts for his expenses out of the partnership account, he admitted that he was unable to get the picture off the ground. Our "honest" producer, of course, returned the investment monies minus the amounts used for his expenses. Not one of the limited partners had any claim, because the wise, but basically dishonest producer had stayed well within his legal rights.

For this reason my advice is, NOT to draw any expense monies at the time of pre-production. Wait until the production is on its way and you honestly can justify your expenses. Make it clear to your investors that there is no guarantee that a motion picture will really go in front of the cameras, or to use the industry term "on the floor." Make it clear that no monies will be expended until production time.

A limited partnership must file a certificate with the county clerk in the county where the business has its offices. The partnership must also publish a "certificate of substance" once a week for six successive weeks in two newspapers in the county in which the certificate has been filed.

This way of financing has many similarities with the financing of stage shows. A great number of small, low-budget films use the limited partnership as a method of financing. In this way each partner risks only relatively small amounts of money, and by the same token has at least some guarantee that his investment will be returned even though he may not see a profit.

Self-Financing (Elbow Grease Financing)

Also called either "credit card financing" or "put-your-money-where-your-mouth-is financing," it is at times the only way for a new filmmaker to get his product from his heart and soul onto the screen. Basically, such financing is not financing at all, but rather the cooperation of many talents. Usually the scriptwriter, the director, the cinematographer and several actors pool their meager resources. It is the type of filmmaking where you spend money on raw stock, laboratory cost and equipment rental only.

Everything Else Must Come Free. Unfortunately, many a promising project washed up on the rocks of failure because of much enthusiasm and little business sense. Such an elbow grease financed film will cost you between $50,000 and $75,000. There are no ifs, ands, or buts about it. For this reason every one of the partners should not only have talent and skill in his respective field, but should be able to invest about $5,000. The rest should come in Limited Partnership Agreements from friends and relatives.

The filmmakers actually involved in the film may bring in their share by personal loan, savings accounts (now severely depleted), or the pledge of monthly installments derived from the 9 to 5 job. Naturally, all should be part of the Limited Partnership.

It is best to have enough capital to complete the picture. If not, have at least enough money to bring the production up to a fine cut in the workprint, including sound and at least some sound effects. In this way you are able to screen your film to prospective distribution companies who hopefully will come in with the required monies to finish the picture.

In case you are unable to attract any limited partners, set yourself a shooting schedule and budget, and just accumulate as much money as needed for each step. Once you have completed step one, save again for step two and so on.

1. Raw stock and costs for developing and printing (also equipment rental costs)
2. Editing equipment and some incidentals

3. Sound work: Music cutting
                   Dialogue cutting
                   Sound effects cutting
4. Mix and transfer of soundwork. At this stage you will be able to screen your picture for prospective distributors.
5. Negative cutting
6. Answer print (a very sizable sum)

You will notice, the steps listed entail only the those elements which require lab work. All other elements—the *elbow grease,* the hard work, the blood and the sweat—must be provided by you. It's fun and it will work. I know.

Chapter Two

The Prospectus

Even a low-budget film is big business. The major stumbling block for many new producers has been the preparation of a professional financial presentation. More than one potentially successful movie did not get off the ground because the prospectus soliciting investments had been non-professional. Remember, your prospectus is the key element to stimulate interest among potential investors.* A clear and well-organized presentation will give your potential investors a better understanding of the motion picture you have planned, and of your own business capabilities. Both should satisfy them that the planned venture will result in a commercial film.

The Professional Look of Your Prospectus

Your presentation should be typed in a good-sized business typeface, and bound into a plastic spiral binder (you will find these in any large stationery store). The title of your project and the name of your film should be heat-stamped on the cover. Do not ruin the clarity of your front cover by embellishing it with either graphics or the stamp "confidential." Both will mark you as an amateur and beginner.

The first page should show a Xerox copy of your business certificate. It is important to file such a certificate stating the fictional name of your company before entering any business venture. The next page is the cover page which gives the following information:

Name of film, adding: "A MOTION PICTURE PROJECT"
Name of production company
Production financing outline

I prefer to add an index on page four. Such an index is not necessary, but usually helpful. Your index should contain the following key elements:

Synopsis
Project Status
Development Plan
Budget

---

*Keep in mind as you are selling "units" to investors that you are offering a "limited partnership" only. Be sure to check with your attorney to steer away from SEC and state securities violations.

Marketing plan
Investors' protection
Sample of investment contract

Synopsis

The synopsis, or the story line of your movie, should not be longer than two, or at the most three pages. It should cover the main elements and the theme of your project in a concise and precise manner. Since it is the part of your presentation that whets the potential investor's appetite, you may do well to have the synopsis written by a professional ad writer. Such a person will bring out the marketable gist of your story. Often the screenwriter himself is too involved with the script to recognize its marketable points. I should advise against submitting the script during the "offering phase" of any negotiations. Few people have time to read scripts, and even fewer know how to read a motion picture script. Submitting a script will only confuse the issue, and lessen your chance of selling a unit. Do not offer your script unless especially requested by the potential investor.

Project Status

Here you will describe how far your project has been developed.

Script: Is a script available? Is the script finished or does it need revisions? Has the scriptwriter a track record?

Director: Has a director been committed, and do you have a contract with him, or a letter of intent? If you have these documents, attach Xerox copies. List all the films that the director has to his credit.

Producer/Production Manager: Since the producer on most low-budget films also functions as production manager, you should list your own expertise in the field. What is your own track record? Have you worked on low-budget features before? Do you have the ability to provide maximum production values on the given budget? Do you have access to expert crew members? Do you know how to cut corners and still bring in a viable project? Do you have connections to post-production facilities? Are you knowledgeable about locations?

Stars: If you have a letter of intent from a well-known star, attach it.

Actors: If you have any actors committed, list their credits.

Financing: If any portion of the budget has been raised through either lab or location deferment and/or participation, list it here.

Production Team: If any key members of your production team such as the cinematographer, editor and art director have been committed, list their credits and strong points.

14

Development Plan

This section describes specific schedules you intend to adhere to during the times of pre-production, production and post-production. This schedule should also show when monies will be spent. A reasonable schedule will include these time elements:

Three months:

Polishing the script in conference with the director.
Location scouting.
Conferences with set-director, special effects person, stunt coordinator.
Initial casting of actors.
Final preparation of budget.

Two months:

Final casting of actors.
Initial meeting with editor and composer.
Contract post-production facilities to be used.
Rehearse actors.
Contract locations, props, sets, special effects and/or start building some.
Order raw stock.
Order equipment (lights, cameras).

One month:

Shoot picture.

One month:

Finish assembly of workprint.

Three months:

Edit workprint.
Edit sound (dialog and sound effects).
Edit music.
Mix and foley.

One month:

Negative cutting.
Optical soundtrack.
Timing of answer print.
Answer print.

Budget

Your budget is the backbone of your presentation. It should be as specific and accurate as possible, and should be realistic enough to give your investors the confidence that you will bring in the film on budget. For this reason, it should be neither too low nor too high. In any event, since your budget is a "proposed" budget, it will require some adjustments shortly before shooting. Still, you will stick as closely as possible to the proposed amounts, making sure your budget will not "blossom." It is fairly easy not to go over budget if you:

1. Have researched all expenditures during the pre-production period.
2. Have received contracts on all expenditures such as lab, location and post-production fees.
3. Have established "ceilings" for equipment and expendables.
4. Make certain that each and every expenditure has to be approved by you.

Budgets are cats of many different breeds. The ones labored over by major studios resemble a best-seller in plumpness, and the ones sent out into the world by hopeful, would-be producers might be meager one page affairs. For the low-budget feature film, you will do well to show a budget of manageable size and content. There are various stock forms available in stationery stores in Hollywood and New York. Over the years, I have developed a form that I am comfortable with, and you might want to adopt it. The numbers given on the budget refer to the numbers used by major studios. I retained the numbers for easier reference.

Account Number	Category	Rate	Totals
101	Writers		
103	Secretarial Expense		
	Mimeograph/Copy Work		
201	Producer		
202	Director		
	Assistant Director		
	Stunt Coordinator		
301	Stars		
	Weekly Players		
	Daily Players		
	Overtime		
	Travel Mileage		
	Looping		
	SAG Pension/P&H Contribution		
302	Extras		
	Stand-ins		
501	Production Manager		
	Assistant Production Manager		
	Script Supervisor		
601	Cameraman		
	Assistant Cameraman		
	2nd Assistant Cameraman		
602	Sound Mixer		
	Boom Man		
603	Art Director/Set Decorator		
	Assistants		

Account Number	Category	Rate	Totals
604	Makeup (Key)		
	Hairdresser (Key)		
	Assistants		
605	Wardrobe Mistress		
606	Key Grip		
	Best Boy		
607	Gaffer		
	Assistant Gaffer		
608	Prop Man		
701	Camera Rentals		
	Camera Purchases and Supplies		
702	Sound Rentals		
703	Set Dressing Rentals		
	Set Dressing Construction		
	Purchases and Supplies		
	Set Dressing Damages		
704	Wardrobe Rentals		
	Wardrobe Purchases		
705	Make-up/Hair Rentals		
	Make-up/Hair Purchases & Supplies		
706	Grip Equipment Rentals		
	Dolly Rentals		
	Grip Purchases & Supplies		
707	Electrical Equipment Rentals		
	Electrical Purchases & Bulbs		
	Electrical Equipment Damages		
708	Property Rentals		
	Property Purchases		
	Property Damages		
709	Picture Car Rentals		
	Picture Car Purchases		
710	Special Effects		
801	Film Editor		
	Assistant Editor		
	Editing Room Rentals		
	Editing Equipment Rentals		
	Editing Purchases		
803	Sound Editor		
804	Music Editor		
805	Projections		
901	Raw Stock		
902	Negative Cutting		
903	All Processing (including answer print & optical track)		
904	Opticals		
905	Titles		
1001	Music Score		
1002	Canned Music Rights		
1003	Sound Effects		
	Sound Effects Transfers		

Account Number	Category	Rate	Totals
1101	1/4 Mag Tape Purchase		
	35 mm Mag Stock Purchase		
1102	Foley		
1103	Transfer Post-Production		
1104	Projection w/Mixer		
1105	Looping		
1106	Dubbing		
1201	Mobile Dressing Rooms		
1202	Trucks & Trailers		
	Prop Van		
	Grip Truck		
	Camera Truck		
	Water Truck & Driver		
1204	Gas/Oil/Maintenance		
1301	Location Rentals		
1302	Police, Fire Marshall, Welfare Worker		
1303	Catering		
	Coffee, Cold Drinks, Snacks		
1305	Overnight Location—hotel		
1306	Overnight Location—per diem, transportation		
1401	Stillman		
1402	Film & Processing		
1403	Public Relations		
1601	Liability Insurance		
	Workmen's Compensation		
	Rented Vehicle Insurance		
1602	Unemployment Tax		
1603	MPAA		
1701	Legal Fees		
1702	Accounting Fees		
1703	Film Shipping		
1704	Telephone and Telegraph		
1805	Petty Cash		
1806	Printing Stationery & Office Supplies		
1901	Salaries for Stuntmen		
	Special Equipment for Stunts		
	Medical Expenses for Minor Injuries		

Using the suggested format you will have about ten to nineteen pages of budget. The first numbers listed under *Account Number* refer to the page on the budget, the last two numbers refer to specific categories.

Once you have produced several movies, you will need a pre-production budget. This should include:

Producer's fee
Director's fee
Writer's fee
Telephone and office rent
Location scouting
Options for stars
Legal fees

Marketing

Here you will emphasize the strengths of your competitive position. You will stress your picture's marketability for home video, cable TV, and syndication, besides the more traditional release areas of foreign and domestic distribution. You will emphasize your ability to bring in a technically and artistically sound picture for far less than any major studio, since you are not burdened with studio overhead and interest charges. These charges do not add anything to the market value of any picture, while adding considerably to its cost. You will add the fact that many members of your production team, while highly qualified and experienced, are not yet union members. Therefore, their salaries are more in keeping with the demands of a low-budget film.

Most of all, you will stress the fact that you have a solid distribution deal. No independent producer, may he be a fledgling or an experienced movie maker, should face the rigors of financing a project without the brace of a distribution deal. Most investors will be hesitant to negotiate if such a deal is not on the books. If your distribution deal is with a company that has a proven record of releases, by all means mention it prominently. It should be helpful if you give information about the company's commitment to prints and advertising, and its schedule of accounting. You should add a Xerox copy of the distribution firm's letter of intent, or (even better) actual commitment, and have a release date ready. Let's assume that you were unable to garner a distribution deal. In this case, you will have to convince your potential investors that you intend to make a far more favorable deal once the picture's workprint is available.

Should you intend to distribute your picture yourself (and it has been done successfully), you'll have to demonstrate your expertise in this field. You must map out a release pattern and advertising campaign. The following items should be covered in this segment of your presentation:

- Agreements with territorial distributors.
- Suggested advertising campaign, including radio spots, trailers, and sheets and flyers.
- Number of prints to be released.
- Proposed release pattern (areas and territories).
- Viability of your proposed plan, specifically how your picture will be targeted to certain markets, and why it should be successful in these markets.

You should be entirely honest and frank as to the risks your potential investors will face investing in any motion picture. Make it clear that your investors might risk losing their investment, and should not invest unless they are financially able to absorb a loss. Point out that the return of any investment will be slow and spread out over a couple of years, as the film will be "bicycled" around the country. This may prove to be a deterrent to some investors, and an incentive to others. Some may welcome the chance of a tax write-off.

Once you have honestly pointed to the negative aspects of motion picture investing, you have your road clear to show off the positive side. Presently the home video market is booming and is expected to increase during the next few years. This product absorbing market is tailor-made for the low-budget film. You may do well to stress the following points in your presentation:

- Home video rights are immediate money, as the rights to produce home video tapes are being sold on a "cash and carry" basis.
- Home video is a quickly expanding market.
- The major studios and big independents are not able to fill the demand for home video.
- Home video is big business domestically as well as overseas.

Secondly, mention the lucrative TV syndication market for low-budget films, as well as the equally booming market for non-theatrical release, such as armed forces theatres, navy ships, cruise ships, governmental agencies, schools and colleges. Thirdly, you should indicate the ever strong foreign market. There are many countries in this world relying on the movie theatre for popular entertainment. These countries still buy movies practically sight unseen, ordering so many horror films and so many suspense/action films, after having viewed maybe ten minutes of each feature. These foreign movie buyers have been, and are still, the backbone of the low-budget film. They are unable to afford the fees demanded by the major studios and big independent companies and have to gravitate to the low-budget film producer.

Investor Protection
You should specify that funds obtained will be held in an escrow account until the film goes into production. If the film should fail to go into production, all monies will be returned.

You might want to alleviate any hesitant investor's fear by supplying a completion bond. The cost of such a bond is approximately 8% of the final budget, and at times it is beneficial to have one in order to attract investors more easily.

You should give the name of the bank you will be dealing with and you should let your investors know whether or not all checks will have to be co-signed.

It is customary to furnish your investors with monthly statements, showing the monies expended and giving a progress report on the film. At the end of the venture, you should give your investors the opportunity to have your books audited by an accountant of their choice.

Sample of Investment Contract

Have your attorney draw up a sample contract covering what your investors will receive in exchange for their money, and how their monies will be protected. This contract should also spell out that your company is not giving any guarantees as to either the recoupment of the monies, or to any profits to be made by the investors.

Chapter Three
Distribution

Every producer needs the distributor to get his film "on the road." The distributor is the one who gets the film into the theatres. He advertises the film and he collects the monies. No matter how excellent the producer's film may be, the final success of it depends to a large degree upon two elements: the *distributor's* sales force and advertising campaign and the *exhibitor's* presentation.

When we look at the totem pole of distribution, we first notice the majors, companies such as Universal, Warners, 20th Century-Fox and Columbia Pictures who handle most of the major motion pictures shown in this country. While up to about fifteen years ago these companies produced and distributed primarily their own films, they now serve mostly as distribution arms for a number of powerful independent production companies. They also serve as the "underwriting" source for said companies. These majors release their motion pictures nationwide. Their pictures are being exhibited in thousands of key theaters during a period of one to twelve months, depending on the success of each film. They rent their films on a percentage base only. A top film will play between 5000 and 10,000 playdates* then it will be pulled out to be leased to cable and later on to network television. Nowadays the major companies will not go after the small circuits. Their overhead cost is so enormous that sending their films to the proverbial "Pete's Drive-In Upper-Mountain-Forge" simply would mean a loss of revenue for them.

Next on the totem pole we see the "mini-majors," all distribution companies that have a strong flow of medium budget films** and have developed distribution facilities handling about twenty branch offices throughout the country.

And last, but not least, is a host of small distribution companies who "bicycle" their films from territory to territory. They depend on multiple releases, playing their films one area at a time. For instance they may play "High School Terror" in fifty theatres in the Los Angeles area, including theaters in outlying districts as far as San Bernardino and Ventura County. After the film has played one playdate in each theatre it will be moved to Atlanta, and from there, say, to Denver. Usually they play their film in multiples of fifty or thirty-five. This practice saves great amounts on shipping as well as advertising costs, which, as we will learn later on in this chapter, can shoot sky high.

*A playdate constitutes the "run" of the film, which might be one week, three days, or even one day.
**Nowadays a "medium" budget film may go up to ten million.

22

Before we proceed any further, let's get acquainted with the basic concepts of distribution, and let's learn how it works. Since the highly complex hierarchy of major studio distribution is beyond the scope of this book, we will concentrate our efforts on the mini-majors and small distribution companies. You will have to rely on the following sources to get your picture into the theaters:

Distribution company—
> Territorial distribution company—
> (also called sub-distributor)
>> Exhibitor—

It might be a good idea to acquaint yourself with the various distribution companies. Take a look at the special issues of the trades such as "Hollywood Reporter," "Variety" and "Box Office" being published for the film markets in Cannes, Milan and Los Angeles, and you will find an excellent overview of distributors. While some of the small companies have been in business as long as the majors, there is still a great number of firms who emerge one season, only to be gone the next.

Distribution

The first-time producer signing with a distribution company will usually sign for "worldwide release." That is to say, the distributor will market your picture domestically (within the borders of the United States) as well as overseas. He will offer your picture to Europe, the Middle-East, Asia, Africa, and other places you did not even dream existed.

If you, with stars in your eyes, are marketing your first picture, the distributor interested in your film is likely to suggest a contract for "worldwide representation in all areas." I would like to suggest that you do not sign such a contract. Try to keep all non-theatrical exhibition (cable, TV, home-video) separate. If you give a distribution company the right to represent your film in all areas, you will lose control over your picture. I know it sounds very tempting to have one firm handle all areas of sales. By the time you have found your first distributor you are tired of all the hassle, all the screenings you had to sit through, all the letters you had to write, all the telephone calls you had to make. Now you have—finally—found someone who likes your film, the product of much work, many sleepless nights and so much love and effort expended. You are ready to sign a contract—any contract, no questions asked. You are afraid your precious distributor might ride off into the sunset if you were not to agree to his terms.

It is by far better to shop patiently around for a distributor who will market your film theatrically, domestically and overseas, another one who only handles TV and cable sales, and a third one who specializes in the home video markets. Often your "worldwide in all areas" distributor has to look for these secondary distributors anyway. He has to pay them a percentage, monies which will eventually come out of your pocket.

Once the theatrical contract has been signed, the distributor is responsible to get your film exhibited. He has to advertise the film and he has to have sufficient release prints on hand. He will advance you the money for the following items:

1. Advertising materials
2. Release prints.*

Of course it is the distributor who will design the advertising campaign and whose advertising department is responsible for the procurement of all needed items. You do not have to worry about any of the advertising materials at this point. You only have to pay for it eventually. Later on we will discuss details and intricacies of advertising, suffice it to say at the moment that for even a very small low-budget film these may run between $5000 to $8000.

The highest item to be advanced is the cost of the release prints. These prints are not inexpensive. Even having them printed at a lab known for its reasonable prices, with a discount, these prints will run slightly over $1000 each. At this point we will not even consider the fact that after a number of showings these prints need to be cleaned, that after more showings they are obsolete and have to be replaced. No, at this moment we only take a deep breath as we realize that we are already between $35-$50,000 in the red if the distributor goes for a multiple release. Adding to this amount the cost of initial advertising will make you reach very quickly for the aspirin bottle and a glass of water.

All right, by now you have recovered slightly and you are strong enough to file the knowledge that it is *you* who has to pay back the advanced money out of your producer's share and you are ready to delve more deeply into the mysteries of distribution.

The first step your distributor will take is to order one or two release prints and to run your picture at trial dates and sneak previews. There are two reasons for these trial dates. First of all, and very obviously, they show whether your picture is commercial. If it proves to be of commercial calibre, then he has to decide in which markets your picture might sell best. Your picture might be a youth-oriented film perfectly right for summer release, or it might be an action film or a shocker geared for mass audience. Possibly your film might not sell in these areas at all, but might find an appreciative audience in the small, but lucrative art market. After your distributor has established the parameters of your feature, he will design the ad campaign and will decide on the territorial distributor. Here he will pick a *sub* (sub-distributor) who has a large number of theatres right for your type of film.

*The film as it is shown in the theatre.

The next step your worldwide distributor will undertake is to offer your film to a territorial distributor, or as they are called in the industry, a "sub." First the film will be leased on a percentage basis. The distributor will get a certain percentage from every dollar earned in the theatre. If the film is being handled on a "sliding scale" these percentage deals can prove to be highly complicated as far as the majors are concerned. In such a deal the distributor's share rises and the exhibitor's scale falls, depending on the popularity of the film. While the majors would more than likely go for a 50-50 deal, it may happen that they end up getting 90% of the house if the film is a blockbuster and plays for weeks on end in the same theatre. Yet it is highly unlikely that your small low-budget film is even being considered on a sliding scale. Here it is the theatre owner, or as he is called in the industry, the *exhibitor*, who earns the lion's share.

Based on one dollar, the breakdown will look as follows:

- The exhibitor will retain 70% of the house,* or he keeps 70 cents out of the dollar.
- 30%, or 30 cents, will be turned over to the distribution company who in turn will pay the sub his share. This share depends to a large degree upon the amount of advertising cost the sub has participated in. The sub usually requires 50% of the producer's share which means he gets 15 cents out of every dollar and the distributor retains 15 cents.
- More than likely the distribution company has offered you a 40-60 deal. You will receive 60% out of the distributor's share and he will retain 40% which would come out to 9 cents per dollar for you.

Of course this sounds like a fair deal, and if you have your first picture on the market, it probably is. Remember, it is the distributor who takes a chance. He has to pay the initial cost of advertising and release prints. He might lose his Gucci shirt representing your little film. Considering the fact that a very conservative amount of revenue for your picture is between $2000 to $4000 a playdate, and also considering that your picture will play domestically about 500 playdates at least, you might be ready to call your favorite travel agency to book a trip around the world. You may even be tempted to scan the real estate section of your paper, to find some good buy in a larger house. Heck, those are only the monies rolling in for domestic release. The foreign market has not even been tapped, and there is TV and cable, and the very lucrative home video market. Well—

—don't count your chickens before they are hatched. Remember the distributor advanced you the money for advertising and release prints. You have to pay that money back. You have to pay the piper. But there is more to come.

* House refers to the money the movie theatre took in for one play date.

25

You the producer are responsible for shipping and local advertising charges (radio spots and newspaper ads). The next item on your list of "distributor's deductions" are the telephone calls he made on behalf of your film. You'll have to pay for all the monies advanced.

It is easy to see that given the percentage participation, you won't see any money for a long, long time even though your film may be successful and may be on a first run basis for two years or longer. The unfavorable percentage deal is the reason why so many producers, after they have given their "blood, sweat and tears" so their dream child may see the screen, will disappear from the scene. They simply could not afford to lose any more of their own and their investor's money. Yes, there are many one-time producers around. There are a few two-timers, but once you have your third and fourth picture to your credit, you have a reasonable chance to survive. By then you have learned the ropes, you have paid your dues and you will avoid pitfalls. The producers who have found ways to make a little money on their films insist on:

1. First dollar participation contract.
2. Flat rate contract.

First Dollar Participation Contract

In a first dollar participation contract you will retain a fraction of the offered percentage. You will retain only about 15-20% of the offered 40-60 deal. But these monies are *yours*, they must be paid to you. From the remaining percentage, say 40-45%, the distributor will reimburse himself for the money he advanced you, and of course he retains the 40% distribution fee as in a standard distribution deal. The deal will revert then to a 50-50 deal, as soon as your debt on the advanced money is paid off.

Flat Rate Contract

You will receive a flat rate, say between $50-250 for each playdate the picture plays. In this contract you will be given the flat rate regardless of whether your picture played in $7000 or $165. In such a contract you will not participate in any advertising cost (radio and newspaper). At times, a deal may be negotiated so that:

1. You will return to a percentage basis once your debts on release prints and initial advertising have been paid off.
2. You remain on a flat rate basis, and do not have to pay back the monies advanced to you.

Once you have several pictures to your credit, you should go for the negative pick-up contract. At least try to receive an advance for the picture. In this case you are certain the film will be distributed.

Distribution Timing

Timing is another important area in which your distributor will be helpful. He knows what films play best in certain areas at certain times. Several years ago summer was the best time for the small low-budget

26

producer to get his product on the market. Things have changed a little, and now many drive-ins have been snapped up by the mini-majors for the important vacation season. If you have a small picture which plays the "heartlands" of the United States and is staple fare for "Pete's Drive-In" then all year round release is your cup of tea. If you have a strong action picture or a frankly youth-oriented picture, then your distributor will make all efforts to have it seen during the summer vacation. At times your picture may even be exhibited in rather prestigious urban multiple screen theatres during the six weeks prior to the important Christmas and Easter releases when all the majors and mini-majors hold back on their products and the exhibitors are strapped for films.

Once your picture has run its course as a "first run feature," it still has a healthy life ahead as a "second feature." The monies taken in on such playdates may run as low as $50 to $100 flat rent for the film. Of course your distributor will participate in this amount with his percentage of the distribution fee. But by then, it's more than likely you will have paid off your debts to him, and since a second feature does not participate in any advertising cost, you the producer will see a pleasant trickle of money. You may count on about 200 to 300 playdates of your film as second feature.

Territorial Distributors

All through the country your distributor will do business with *subs*. These territorial distribution companies are exactly what their name implies. They have certain territories which they supply with films. These territories usually cover a fairly wide area. A Los Angeles based "territorial" may include some Western states such as Colorado and New Mexico as well as Arizona within its territory. A big Chicago-based territorial may supply the entire Midwest with its films. Of course there are numerous smallish territorials who may do business within one state or several cities.

The question is obvious: Why can't you, the producer, deal with these territorials directly? Why can't you sell to them and forget about the worldwide distributor? The answer is not easy. Of course you can self-distribute your film. There is no law prohibiting this practice. After having been in the film business for a while you know the territorials to trust. You know who is reliable, who has good theatres and most importantly, who will take a chance on a small low-budget feature.

Yet, if you work directly with a territorial distributor, it is you who has to pay for the release prints, the initial advertising cost and the distributor's share of local advertising. Unlike the worldwide distributor, the territorial *will not* advance you any money. Of course you may offer him a flat rate contract, but it is unlikely that he will agree to such a contract if your film is "first run," since he would have to pay for release prints and the initial advertising campaigns. The only way to get a flat rate contract is to have your picture on a double bill as a second feature. At times a territorial may go for such a deal, especially if he wants to double it with a first run picture that is not terribly strong and needs a back up. You may only go for such a deal if you feel your revenues will come in through foreign and home video sales—both areas will bring in higher dollars if you have a US domestic release.

After you have produced several pictures you might want to go into "self-distribution." You should shy away from the big territorials. Your best bet is to find some small local distributors whom you know to be honest and hard-working. These people in turn will be able to recommend some of their friends who handle various territories. These territorials do not work out of exclusive offices; they are the true shirt sleeve salesmen. They go out into the sticks and sell. Most of their business is located in the Midwest, South and Southwest. They sign a contract with the local theatre owner while they treat him to lunch at "Mom's Diner." Their films never play in the key or even sub-key areas, but in all the small towns across the country. Of course, during the past few years, since audiences became more demanding, and since the advent of cable, many of these small theatres have been forced to close down. Still their numbers are large enough for a sizable amount of small time distributors. If you work with these companies, of course you will have to pay for your release prints and advertising. However, these costs will be relatively small. It might be sufficient if you initially offer five to ten release prints. You will have to supply an attractive one sheet and some slicks and pressbooks. The cost for radio and small town local newspaper advertising is not exorbitant, and might to some degree be shared with the exhibitor.

Distributing in such a manner, you should go in for a 50-50 deal. You demand 50% of the house (or floor, as it is termed in some areas), meaning you get 50% of what the theatre grosses. You in turn will pay the territorial an agreed upon fee—usually about 15% of your dollar earnings.

Four Walling

Four walling simply means that you, the producer, go out, rent a theatre, pay the exhibitor's staff, pay for the advertising of your film and take in the entire "floor." This practice sounds very lucrative and it sounds easy. But, it isn't. Even though some low-budget film producers have seen considerable success in "four walling," there are others who went broke. Even on a very small scale "four walling" is not only an expensive, but also a time consuming proposition. It is you who has to rent the theatre, oversee the shipping of the print, collect the money—each and every one a harassing detail costing you time and energy, as well as money.

If you have a good and reliable distributor, let him do the distribution. He is an expert in his field, he knows what to do and what not to do. Let him worry about the many facts connected with distribution. It is far better for your soul and credit rating if you concentrate on your next project.

Foreign Distribution

Your picture is playing domestically. Now you glance overseas for added "fame and fortune," and of course, revenue. Starting out as a new kid on the block you have probably signed with a distributor for overseas as well as domestic release. If your distributor is a company of some stature and importance it will probably show your picture at all, or at least some of the important international film markets:

Los Angeles (March)
Cannes (April)
Milan (October)
Manila (October)

A great number of film markets, film fairs and film festivals take place all over the world during any given month of the year. But only the above mentioned markets are the ones drawing buyers from around the world. During the past years, the Asian film industry has become a strong competitor for the American film. Still, the American film (even your low-budget feature) is the one most foreign buyers want to screen.

The most important markets for the low-budget film producer are the ones in Milan and Los Angeles. The Cannes market is the most prestigious one. Yes, it is the most glamorous and most advertised one. Yet Cannes caters mostly to the majors and the big independents. Being represented in Cannes is more or less a matter of prestige. You will make your best sales in Milan and Los Angeles. The Manila market is less important for the American filmmaker, as it concentrates on the work of Asian producers.

It goes without saying, you will not go to any of these film markets. The cost would be prohibitive. Your distributor, who represents your film along with a dozen other features, will go. He is responsible for paying for all his expenses, rental of booths, transportation, lodging and food for himself and his staff, advertising slicks for your film, cost of ads in the major trade papers such as "Variety," "Hollywood Reporter," "Box Office" and various foreign publications. He will not ask you for any money in advance. You will agree with me that his fee, between 30% to 40% of the sale of your picture, is at least somewhat justified.

You have to supply him with a 3/4" video tape of your film. At the markets, films are shown continuously on a number of television screens. Buyers wander from booth to booth, watching part of the films, picking up flyers, arguing, and hopefully buying.

The practice of foreign distribution is far different from domestic distribution. First of all you will go for neither a percentage nor a flat rate deal. The reason for this is obvious. Your distributor has no way of checking the "floors" (income) of the theatres overseas. The common practice is to arrange an outright sale to any foreign territory. The distributor will supply the foreign distributor with a negative of your film (for which the buyer has to pay) as well as some one sheets and ad materials. For a fixed sum, the foreign distributor can cut as many release prints as he wishes. The rate paid for films varies greatly. While the sums for major films go into the millions, you might have to be satisfied with fees ranging between $2,500 to $10,000 per foreign country.

Once you have your feet at least a little "wet" in this business (let's say you have about three films to your credit), you should make every effort to sign with one distributor to represent your film domestically, and with a different one for foreign release. Never, and I repeat this, *never* sell your film yourself as far as the foreign market is concerned. This is a field only to be tackled by an expert. Foreign sales are fraught with difficulties. The seller has to deal with import regulations that will vary from country to country. Some countries will buy your film but will not permit any money to leave their borders. You literally have to pick up your cash yourself. Others will not permit certain elements in your film. Others have to approve the import of your film, and so on and on ad nauseam. Once a sale has been consummated, an LC (letter of credit) will be made out to you. Only after you hold this letter will you ship the film to the respective buyer. After several more weeks the LC will clear and you will be rewarded with heavenly cash. The time element from initial sales contract to final check will take anywhere from four to seven months.

Auxiliary Markets

Auxiliary markets, also called non-theatrical markets, encompass TV (network and syndicated), cable and home video sales. In these areas (excepting network which will not be receptive to your product) you, the low-budget film producer, will see some fairly good money. Most importantly, this money will be received comparatively soon after the initial sale. As mentioned before, you should make every effort to keep all non-theatrical rights to your film. Get in touch with a distributor who deals in these areas exclusively. Here is a word of warning: even if you are fully convinced of your distributor's integrity and honesty, do not give him access to either the negative or answer print of your film. It is true that they do need your answer print in order to cut the l-inch master required for home video and television sales, but let the distributor order these tapes through you, the producer. You in turn will supply the distributor with the tape which you ordered at a lab of your choice. The buyer will pay for the cost of the 1-inch tape. Here you have to make certain about the format. Many foreign countries require a tape compatible with the PAL system. The cost of having such a tape recorded will be about $1,000.

You will find the names of distributors specializing in home video and TV in the film market issues of the trades. Incidentally, the way of selling your film for these areas is identical to theatrical sales. You will supply your distributor with a 3/4-inch tape of your film, and he will screen it on a television screen.

The money you will receive in these markets is nice, even if it is not as big as you may have hoped. Remember, you are selling a small low-budget feature, not a multi-million dollar block buster. While it is a fact that home video buyers will pay hundreds of thousands of dollars for even an unimportant major film, they will only spend as little as $2,500 to $10,000 for your film. These sales usually go in "blocks." You will sell to Great Britain, the Scandinavian countries, Australia, (which might include Hong-Kong), and then to countries such as Italy, Germany, France and Spain. It is more lucrative to sell to the two most important territories—Scandinavia and Great Britain—first, and then go down the line to the other countries. These two important buyers might be reluctant to accept your film if they see you have sold to other territories first.

At times, a buyer will suggest that you go for a percentage on each tape sold, plus an advance. Again, I feel this to be too risky, as you will have no control over the number of prints actually cut. It is far better to go for an outright sale. Go for the "sparrow in your hand" and let "the dove on the roof" fly wherever it fancies. Unfortunately, there is a tremendous amount of piracy going on. It is only to be hoped that strong laws will put a stop to this deplorable practice.

There will always be a strong temptation to send your tapes to one of the many buyers advertised in the trades. Even though most of these people are meticulously honest, I would refrain from sending out my tapes. Again, let the distributor handle your sales.* He has learned to avoid pitfalls. (Yet, if for any reason you may see fit to mail out your tapes, make certain you have printed on the tape every so often "DEMO REEL." The lab cutting your 3/4-inch tape will make it foolproof.)

As far as TV is concerned, your film will probably be offered with about fifty other films as a "package." These packages are important for syndicated television. I have a feeling that the packaging of films will become more important as cable audiences expand, and the mechanics of syndication will be taken up by cable. If your film is in such a package you may see as little as $500 a year, or as high as $5,000. But, if you consider that these contracts run between five to seven years, these amounts are nothing to be sneezed at.

Yes, all these amounts seem relatively small, but they will add up in the long run. Also remember, you are saving the cost of expensive advertising, as well as the cost of release prints.

Advertising

Advertising your film is one of the functions of the distributor, whether he represents your film for domestic and foreign theatrical or non-theatrical release. Let's look at advertising the theatrical film for domestic release since this campaign is the most involved and—naturally—the most expensive one.

Advertising and publicity are usually geared towards the audience most likely attracted to a given film. Of course, the monies expended on a film depend on the film's budget. A thirty million dollar blockbuster—even though it may prove to be a "stiff"—will automatically be blessed with a much larger budget than a smaller, comparatively inexpensive film. It doesn't matter at all that the smaller film might be the better one.

Understandably, at this point we are not concerned about advertising campaigns on a national scale. We will focus our attention entirely on the kind of advertising that you, the low-budget producer, have to deal with.

*Your distributor will charge between 20%-30% distribution fee.

The advertising campaign begins many weeks or months before the time the answer print will be completed. As soon as a rough cut is available, the distribution company's copywriter and art director will look at your product and discuss the general advertising approach. If you are dealing with a "one man distributor," it is he who, in concert with you, will agree upon the ad campaign and farm out the jobs of designing and printing one sheets and flyers to the National Screen Service in New York. At this time, the distributor will also cut a five to seven minute demo reel of your yet unfinished film to interest prospective exhibitors. It is the responsibility of the distributor to supply all advertising materials and to advance you the cost. We are looking at the following materials:

One sheets
Slicks
Pressbooks
Lobby display pictures (for the foreign market only)
Radio spots
TV spots
Theatrical trailer

One Sheets
These are the posters you see displayed outside movie theatres. At times, the posters are very attractive, some are even of an artistic calibre, but it's more than likely that they are somewhat on the garish side, and every so often you might find some of particularly poor taste. The distributor will hire an artist to design the artwork—that is to say, the drawing as it is to appear on the one sheet. The cost will be between $1,500-$2,000. Then the poster goes to the printer. Here the cost is determined by the number of colors used. As more colors are used, more "green stuff" goes to the printer. It's as simple as that. Fortunately it really doesn't matter how many colors you display on your one sheet. If the title of your film has draw and the rendering is catchy, your best bet will be a three color poster. At times it may even be more effective to use only two colors.

Slicks
The distributor needs thousands of them, as he will hand them out by the fistful during the various film markets. He will mail them over and over to his prospective clients. A slick is a 8 x 10 version of the one sheet. On the reverse side you'll find the synopsis of your film, along with the names of the lead actors, director and cinematographer. Some distributors like to add one or two production stills.

Pressbooks
A pressbook is another 8 x 10 sheet showing between five to eight increasingly smaller versions of your one sheet, accompanied by some catchy text. These are samples of the ads that the exhibitor will place in his local paper. Since the distributor and the exhibitor share the

newspaper advertising cost, the very size of the ad is often a sore point of contention. Unfortunately, advertising in newspapers is not inexpensive these days, especially since ads for films are higher in price than the equal size ads for other businesses. Ordinary advertising is placed "run of paper;" the newspaper places the ad at its discretion. However, a film ad has to appear on a specific page, and therefore the cost goes up (they claim).

Lobby Display Pictures

These are 8 x 19 black and white glossies that are displayed in movie theatre lobbies to attract the movie-going audience to next week's feature. These displays are outdated as far as the domestic market is concerned, although they are still very popular in most overseas markets.

Radio Spots

Radio spots are another very effective advertising medium for the low-budget film. The knowledgeable distributor, in concert with the exhibitor, will buy radio time according to the audiences he wants to reach. Surveys have shown that many daytime listeners are women going about their chores. For this reason, if a picture seems of special interest to women, the distributor will spend many of his advertising dollars on daytime radio. For an action film or youth oriented picture a very effective time is the slot from 7 to 9 AM and 4 to 7 PM—both rush hour times.

TV Spots

TV advertising is extremely expensive, and therefore more than likely out of reach for your picture. Actually, these spots are 30-second commercials for your film. If such a spot is being considered, it will be cut from your theatrical trailer.

Theatrical Trailer

They are the "teasers" for your film. We all are familiar with the few minutes of film before the feature begins advertising the coming attractions. Usually the distributor will have a trailer cut as soon as the fine cut of your film is completed. Often a mediocre film has drawn at least some audiences by the fine trailer advertising it.

Examination of Records

A satisfactory agreement between the producer and the distributor about accounting is imperative. You have the legal right to audit the distributor's books and records as far as your film is concerned. In order to avoid any upcoming disagreement, your right to audit should be stated in the distribution contract. Basically you should have the right to audit the following records:

Ledgers
Cash receipts
Ledgers pertaining to your film
Bills, vouchers and cancelled checks of charges against the film
Exhibition contracts
Box office reports
Advertising cost
Shipping cost

It usually is wise to make certain in the distribution contract that for the first 18 months accounting will be done on a monthly basis. You will encounter resistance from your distributor who will insist on the usual three month accounting. Still, remain firm. If any discrepancy should be discovered, it is much easier to go after it immediately. The reports should be issued on a country by country and territory by territory basis. All income and all expenses charged against your picture should be reported on the same basis.

Chapter Four

The Screenplay

The Acquisition of Literary Property

Every motion picture is based upon a *property*. This property may be an original screenplay, a book, a stage play, or an article in a magazine or newspaper. The property is the starting point for the entire motion picture process. First, you must determine who owns the rights to the property. Contact the US Copyright Office in Washington D.C. to check whether a copyright has been registered and who the copyright proprietor is. Most authors will register their properties in their name, however some publishers insist upon retaining the copyright. In any event, the prudent producer will deal only with the owner of the copyright. If a property has been published outside the US, it is even more important to check into the copyright. Generally, the property will be protected under the Universal Copyright Convention.

Optioning of Property
Most likely, you will acquire an *option* for between six months to one or even two years for a fee between $500 to $10,000 or more, depending on how well known the book and author are. The low-budget film producer usually pays about $500 for a period of six months and retains the rights to renew the option. If you are lucky enough to be associated with a writer who does not charge any option fee, since he is primarily interested in screen credits and seeing his property made into a feature film, you should still negotiate an option. Money does not necessarily have to be exchanged to obtain an option. Your option agreement should contain a literary purchase agreement that will come into effect as soon as the option is exercised. This agreement should state that the purchase price of the property includes:

- The rights to title, plot, theme and characters.
- The right to utilize the property for television, radio, cable, home video, pay-TV and all other non-theatrical distribution known or unknown at the time of agreement.
- The right to change plot, theme and characters.
- The right to write a synopsis not exceeding 10,000 words, and to promote and advertise the feature film.

The honorarium you will have to pay to the author varies from deal to deal. You may pay as little as $1,000 for the property (at times even including a finished screenplay), but customarily if your picture is below

$500,000 you will pay $5,000 for the property and another $5,000 for the final draft screenplay. Even with Writers Guild regulations there are no hard and fast rules to adhere to. Optioning and purchasing a property and screenplay is, and has always been open to negotiation.

The Screenplay Agreement

It is likely you will hire a screenwriter to write the screenplay based upon the purchased property. In the case of an original screenplay, you have the option to retain the author to rewrite the screenplay to your specifications. In this case, of course, an additional fee is due. The screenplay agreement should provide for all stages of the writing and/or rewriting.

The first stage is called the *synopsis*. This is a short narrative statement of the plot and a description of the main characters. A good synopsis is required for the producer's prospectus.

The second stage is called the *treatment*. Now, the narrative statement of the plot is expanded—there are some sample lines of dialogue, descriptions of locations, and more detailed descriptions of major and minor characters. The average length of the treatment is between 30 to 50 pages.

The third stage is called the *first draft screenplay*. At this point, scenes and dialogue are fully developed and defined. You may expect a first draft screenplay to run between 120 to 150 pages, far too long for the requirements of a low-budget film.

The fourth stage is the rewriting phase. Your main concern at this time is to weed out all over-writing, to eliminate unnecessary characters, and to consolidate locations and events. Though you are concerned about the artistic quality of the screenplay during the first three stages it is not the time to scrutinize it in regards to budgetary requirements.

The final stage of your screenplay is called the *shooting script*. The screenwriter in concert with the director will now indicate each camera setup and will give sound clues in case these are required. Some directors like to work simultaneously on their storyboard.

The Mechanics of the Screenplay

Many would-be writers have great ideas that in the hands of a craftsman would make excellent screenplays. Actors, directors and cinematographers burning with ideas and concepts are submitting scripts in all shapes and forms. Unfortunately, without the basic knowledge about the mechanics of a screenplay all these scripts are ending in the slush pile and many good screenplays are lost forever. Screenplay writing is not only an art, it is also a *craft*.

Only if you are a solid craftsman, will your artistic sparks ignite. You may heed the advice that the artist Delacroix gave to a young painter, "First learn to be a craftsman, it won't keep you from being a genius."

Basically, a screenplay is a story told in pictures. Keep this in mind as you look for the property for your next feature film. Decide whether the story can be translated visually without losing its intrinsic value.

Think in terms of the camera. You cannot tell your audience about conditions. You must show them. Do not permit your actor long tirades about life in the ghetto, but show the over-crowded living quarters, the rats running through the hallways, the garbage rotting in the streets. And of course, you have to decide on a screenplay that is viable for the market you try to reach. Yet, beyond these criteria you may also consider your responsibilities as a manufacturer of a mass media product. Many people will view your film, and a great many may be affected by what is happening on the screen. Your influence upon a worldwide audience is almost beyond comprehension. You may be one of the forces leading people to either good or evil. Besides the obvious reason of entertaining an audience, there must be a deeper commitment to why a picture is being made, to why you put your energy and money, as well as other people's money, into a few rolls of celluloid. This commitment, the true backbone of your film is its *theme*. Your theme is your statement of purpose, the point when you prove something to be true. In this moment of truth the audience will have to face up to themselves, to their emotions and their beliefs. The theme must run through the entire picture, yet not one of your characters should ever mention it. Your theme must be shown pictorially. Remember, *a film is a story told in pictures*.

Let's quickly examine the themes of some famous films, all based on great novels:

"The Grapes of Wrath": the triumph of the human spirit in adversity.
"From Here to Eternity": the insanity of the bureaucratic system.
"The Spy Who Came in From the Cold": man can only depend on himself.

The Three Segments of the Screenplay

Considering the fact that the average feature film will cover the time period of ninety minutes, we know that we have to fit the story into a definite time space. This forces us into an economy of words, economy of story material and economy of characterization. All these economies demand a carefully set up screenplay. In the beginning of the screenplay we set the story premise. In the middle we set the conflicts and obstacles. In the end we set the denouement. Diagrammed, an effective screenplay looks like this:

15 to 20 pages	60 to 80 pages	20 Pages
Beginning (Set up)	Middle (Confrontation)	End (Denouement)

You see, we are looking at a relatively short beginning—just long enough to introduce our audience to the story being told—a comfortable middle where our story unfolds, and a short ending (always remembering that an audience's attention can only be kept for a certain length of time). Once the story has reached its climax, the denouement should be brought forth without much delay.

The above diagram forces us into another demand of the effective screenplay—*graduation*. Let's first examine some faulty handling of graduation.

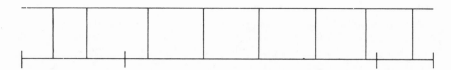

Stagnant Graduation: No event, emotionally, story-wise or picturewise, stands out. The picture has a dulling effect upon the audience. We often find stagnant graduation in relationship stories. In these films all events are handled on either a constantly subtle or a constantly high emotional level.

Uneven Graduation: (A) Events are placed in an illogical order resulting in a disconnected screenplay. Audiences will soon lose interest.

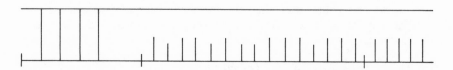

Uneven Graduation: (B) Strong beginning, uninteresting middle, and weak ending. After the audience's interest has been aroused to a high pitch in the beginning, they soon get bored.

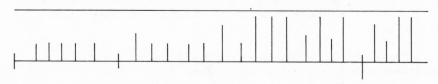

Uneven Graduation: (C) Weak beginning. Interesting graduation starts too late. Audiences will have lost interest before the movie even begins.

Maximum Graduation: The interest of the audience is aroused immediately, but not by events which are so impressive as to prevent subsequent graduation. After giving the audience a "rest period" at the onset of the middle section, each event rises in importance and intensity, leaving increasingly shorter rest periods until we reach a quick and high intensity end.

Graduation must be applied to every element in the story. Every characterization must grow and become clearer toward the end. Every emotion must gain in strength, every decision must become graver, every event more fascinating. In this respect it is important that each element in the story is strengthened. Events cannot be escalated without characterization and emotion in concert. For this reason the writer should only choose characters and emotions that lend themselves to strengthening. Since no such strengthening can be achieved from weak motives the goals chosen have to carry graduation. The strengthening of characterization and emotion should come gradually, without undue jumps. The highest point of all graduation should be reached at the end of the picture.

The technique of graduation applies to all motion pictures, no matter whether they be horror films, adventure-suspense epics, or stories based upon human relationships. Eugene Vale phrases it correctly when he writes: "Our subconscious receptiveness acts with the same precision as the photographic film. It records the values of each scene with a precise sense of graduation. If there is a stagnation or even revision of the progress it will leave a blank on our receptive minds."* The audience reaction will be boredom and disinterest.

Looking at the structure of the screenplay, we come to the conclusion that it is, like its sister the stageplay, arranged in three acts. It is true, these acts do not have the definite break found in the traditional stage play. Still, if we examine them closely, we will find each act has a definite beginning, middle and end. In a subtle form, these segments require the same graduation that an entire screenplay demands.

The end of each act is signified by a twist. Some established condition changes, giving way to new information. Or, we may say that at the end of each act the story "changes direction." To illustrate this concept, let's take a look at my script "Voodoo."

A tutor is hired to take care of three children living with a cook and gardener in an isolated area. We are given to understand that their previous governess has left.

* Eugene Vale "The Technique of Screenplay Writing", The Universal Library, Grosset & Dunlap, New York, 1944.

Precisely at the end of Act I a switch lets us suspect foul play—the tutor finds the departed governess' billfold containing a driver's license and credit cards. All through Act II we believe that the poor girl has come to a disastrous end, when at the end of Act II we find that the tutor comes face to face with her. However we do not know if she is real, or if she is a ghost. The climax in Act III supplies the answer.

Some Guidelines For Effective Screenplay Writing

The Beginning
The first two items we have to decide upon are:

The Goal
The Counter-goal

The *goal* of the protagonist (hero) is the agitating force of the screenplay. The goal must be achieved in the future, because it is not possible to experience fear or hope in regards to something that happened in the past. The goal must be something that almost everyone can identify with. It is vitally important that the goal is brought in early. Without a goal to move it forward, your screenplay will stand still. The goal should never be vague. It must be clear in the writer's and the audience's minds.

We distinguish between three basic types of goal:

- The positive goal: Rita wants to marry John.
- The negative goal: Rita's father wants to prevent the marriage.
- The split goal: John wants to marry Rita, and he wants to sell his screenplay.

Many new writers do not recognize the danger of the split goal. Looking at it, you can easily see that you have two different stories on hand—the goals have nothing in common. The split goal happens most often in action scripts that also require a love story. You should try to bring both goals as close together as possible. How about: John *must* write a selling screenplay to win over his competitor for Rita's hand, *but* he only can write a terrific screenplay if he can marry Rita. I admit that this is not a prize-winning story, but it will illustrate the point I want to make.

The goal requires the protagonist's action, and all incidents in Act II must have their roots in the goal established in Act I. Yet, no goal can be envisioned without the proper *motive*. Or to put it differently, there must be a connection between cause (motive) and effect (goal). No action is possible without a motive. A man walking across a desert must have a motive for doing so—he must have a goal in his mind. If the screenwriter fails to establish these two most crucial points in the audience's minds, then—no matter how exciting the hero's adventures are, no matter how well graduated all the incidents have been written—he will fail to arouse the audience's interest and empathy.

It will help your screenplay immensely if you can present your audience with a countergoal. For instance: Two men make their way through the desert. Ahmed wants to warn his friends, the Foreign Legionnaires, about impending danger. Ishmahed wants to blow up the group of soldiers. Ahmed has to reach them before Ishmahed can set his Molotov cocktail into action.

By now you have established the WHAT of your screenplay:

    Motive
    Goal
    Countergoal

Don't forget to check whether or not you have not forgotten the obvious, such as letting your audience know:

    Who
    Where

Remember the three ingredients of basic plot structure:
    WHAT—WHO—WHERE

The moment the goals clash, we have *struggle and conflict.* We are well on our way to Act II, or the middle of our screenplay.

The Middle
The ancient Greek theatre established three reasons for conflict:

    Man against man.
    Man against nature.
    Man against himself.

Well, we did not find any new conflicts. All our own struggles and tribulations have been neatly wrapped up by writers two thousand years ago. Man against man is the most universal conflict, but man against himself is the more interesting one—it leads up to the test of character. To add more depth to any conflict situation we may use the *affinity and repulsion* theory. According to this theory conflict is caused by:

    Separating two poles of affinity (*Romeo and Juliet*).
    Combining the poles of repulsion (*Mr. Roberts*).

A word of warning if you intend to use the affinity and repulsion theory: To keep the poles of affinity separated there must be a strong reason for the separation. Nowadays Romeo and Juliet would get married, regardless of their parents' objections. In medieval Italy they could not consider such a solution to their problem.

41

Also, there must be strong forces to keep the parts of repulsion from splitting. "Mr. Roberts" is such an effective play because not one single man can escape from the ship. A war is going on. Leaving the ship would be desertion.

As you graduate the middle of your screenplay, as events become more dangerous, and countergoals become more sinister, keep in mind that both the goal and countergoal should have equal chance to succeed. If Ahmed and Ishmahel both have to walk twenty miles, if both have to endure thirst and exhaustion, if both have to fight a sandstorm, then our interest is aroused. But, if only Ahmed has to suffer while Ishmahel comes upon a group of Nomads who willingly loan him a camel, we will quickly go out to the lobby to fortify ourselves with popcorn. We know what is going to happen. Why sit and watch what we know anyway? You will devote the entire Act II to your protagonist's sub-goal. That is to say, the steps he takes to reach his goal. Each and every one of the sub-goals must either be satisfied or frustrated. By letting the audience know what happens to the sub-goal we advance the story. Keeping the story moving is your most tedious work in Act II.

The forward movement of a script does not happen by accident. It has to be planned carefully. The sequences of events should be arranged consecutively on the basis of cause and effect. Each event and each scene must:

Give us new information.
Confirm or denounce previously obtained information.
Follow our interest.
Cause anticipation.

In order to achieve the above requirements of forward movement, we simply have to arrange the essential sub-goals in the story in such a way that a new sub-goal starts *before* the previous sub-goal has either been satisfied or frustrated. Let me repeat: *Each sub-goal must be in accordance with the main goal.* Diagrammed, an effective pattern causing high anticipation will look as such:

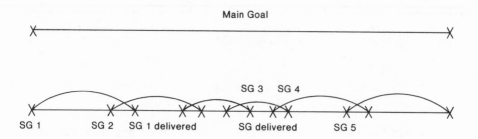

You will notice the way the sub-goals overlap. You will also notice their irregular pattern. In order to illustrate this technique let's look at the "Cinderella Story."

42

MAIN GOAL: She wants to attend the ball.
Sub-goal 1: She must finish her work before she is permitted to
leave.
Sub-goal 2: She must find a suitable dress.
Sub-goal 3: She must find transportation.

You should avoid long stretches without sub-goals. By the same to-ken, you should keep the sub-goals in their proper perspective, never al-lowing them to overshadow the main goal. Your aim will be to structure a story that will steadily increase your audience's interest and raise their feelings of suspense.

Your audience will experience hope and fear, and will eagerly follow the yarn you are spinning, if you give them their full measure of sus-pense. In order to be fearful or hopeful about an event, the spectators have to be able to *anticipate* something. Your audience will feel empathy with the characters on the screen the moment each of your spectators decides the possible outcome of your character's sub-goal.

- We anticipate a certain happening. The event occurs as anticipated—fulfilled expectancy.
- We anticipate a certain happening. Another event takes place—surprise.
- We do not expect anything to happen. An event takes place—shock.

However, as you employ the technique of anticipation do not frag-ment your story by using different viewpoints. Remember, the sub-goals must be pursued by the protagonist. An audience member will experi-ence each event through his own eyes, from his own viewpoint.

The End
Strange as it may seem, your ending is the first thing you must decide upon *before* you even begin your screenplay. It is true, you will be working backwards. Once you know the "hook" of your story, you will find a satisfying or exciting ending. Then, add a plausible beginning, and invent the plot points of Act I and Act II.

A good ending is not easy to come by, it must be *logical* and will state a definite resolution of the problem investigated throughout the screenplay. As you work on your ending ask yourself:

Is the resolution logical?
Is it believable?
Is it clearly stated?
Have I left any questions unanswered?

The ending and the beginning of your screenplay should be related. The ending will answer the question posed in the beginning. But there is more to it. Life moves in a circle. The ending of one thing is the beginning of the next.

Characters Make Your Screenplay Come to Life

The screenwriter is faced with the problem of conveying plausible and lifelike characters to the audience. Unfortunately the requirements of the motion picture represent considerable obstacles to sensitive characterization. In the novel, we know what a character *thinks*. In the feature film we see how he *acts*. A character is built not as much in his dialogue, but in his reactions to situations. Basically, regardless of whether you are writing a suspense or a relationship film, you are faced with the chore of putting your character in increasingly more precarious situations. He proves his character in action, whereby action should be understood in the broader sense of reaction.

Unfortunately, there are many producers who are interested in physical action and deplore all characterization as "highbrow stuff." Yet, action by itself does not exist. Someone must act, and in order to act, this person must have a motive and a goal. We, the audience, must get to know this person, but we will only become interested in him if he is properly characterized. This characterization in turn will determine how he reacts to certain events, and how he acts in order to achieve his goal. It is as simple as that.

In order to have empathy with the character, the audience must know some basic facts about him:

The character's age.
The character's environment.
The character's occupation.
The character's relation to other people.

For the motion picture we must be able to manifest each character's *characteristics*. At times a seemingly unimportant side action reveals more about a character than a long drawn out scene. What do you think about the millionaire who bends down to pick up a penny from a muddy sidewalk? And how about the mother shopping in the supermarket who quickly exchanges some cereal her child needs for a lipstick?

The screenwriter should always be in search of an expressive action that will *reveal* the character. Nothing is too irrelevant to betray a characteristic.

You also may reveal the character by putting him in juxtaposition with other characters. The actions and attitudes of other people with him will give much information. In this manner a character may even be revealed by the reactions of others before he is being introduced to the audience.

Yet, a word of warning: Do not overload your character with characteristics. It is true, in life each of us tends to show chameleon-like character switches. We are many things to many people. The time span of a motion picture is too short to allow such detail. It will serve you well if you give your main character three characteristics *(traits)*. These traits have to complement each other. For minor characters one trait is sufficient.

At times, a writer will assign actions haphazardly, disregarding the fact that action reveals character. If a series of events is the prime interest of his action film, then he must find characters that fit the action he plans. He should realize that different situations and events have different effects upon characterizations.

In action films often there seems to be a preponderance of similar characters showing similar characteristics. Work hard to avoid this. Struggle for contrast, and make each character different. In my film "Hell Riders" we were faced with characterizing two sets of very similar people. One was a gang of bikers, the other one a group of waitresses working in a rural diner. Biker One wore a prison outfit and a Confederate cap. Another one was a defrocked minister, a third one a high school dropout (given to wearing his football helmet), and so on. The waitresses wearing all the same uniform presented a different problem. They could not be characterized visually, but had to have different attitudes. One girl was feisty, the next one docile and sweet, while the third one, with her eye on Hollywood, played the "Vamp."

Try to master the art of characterization. It is fun. In the beginning of the screenplay, as you introduce your characters, do not hit your audience with full blown character studies, but bring in each detail of your characters subtly and constantly. Reveal characters step-by-step, until all factors have been exposed. Secondly, choose combinations of characters that will call forth action.

Character Traits

Even though actors will make the characters that you dreamed about and wrote about come to life, it is your responsibility to present the actors with well-developed characters. You have to endow your characters with *traits*. You will reveal:

Physical traits
Personal traits
Emotional traits

Physical Traits
Physical traits are expressed in the physical make-up of a person. It is true, the director and the producer will search for a person who has exactly the look they want, but the writer is the one who has to define the look. He has to be specific about the physical attributes of the character. Simply to state: "Nancy, his daughter, is a pretty girl," is much too general and doesn't give the director anything concrete to work with. But, "Nancy, his daughter, is endowed with the deceiving softness of a kitten," makes us understand immediately the kind of person that she hides behind the facade of demure sweetness.

Physical traits are effective tools to indicate personal and emotional traits. The audience subconsciously associates looks with character. For instance, Alfie, your meek accountant who is afraid of his own shadow, should not have the physique of a linebacker, and Cheryl your homecoming queen must be a knock-out, not a rotund little tub of lard.

Personal Traits
These are the traits that identify social and ethical qualities: ambitious/lazy, brave/frightened, loyal/disloyal, kind/mean, generous/stingy, thrifty/miserly. You see, the list is endless. Once you have decided upon the physical traits of your character you must either endow him with personal traits that are in accordance or in contrast with his looks.

Emotional Traits
Our emotional traits stem from our physical traits. An attractive person develops different emotional traits than his homely neighbor, and the total of physical and emotional traits often are the cause for personal traits. Take two college students for instance: Lizzy the blonde, blue-eyed California girl with the gorgeous bikini figure is treated by everyone with admiration and kindness. She has an abundance of dates, her teachers treat her kindly and she picks up summer jobs in no time. She knows the world is her oyster. Naturally she is easygoing and has a friendly, sunny disposition. Skinny, big nosed Olive is used to being a wallflower. She knows that no one pays much attention to her. After all, who wants to bother with the likes of her? Naturally, she is reserved, maybe a little bitter and even bitchy at times. It stands to reason that Olive compensates for the lack of personal attention she receives by becoming an A student. You see, the combination of her physical and emotional traits result in her personal trait—ambition.

Character Tags

One of the most efficient ways to bring characters to life is by isolating a dominant *tag* and repeating it. Let's take a look at some of these tags:

Appearance tags
Mannerism tags
Expression tags

Appearance Tags
Give your character some item of clothing, make-up, or a prop that makes him memorable and recognizable. For instance, Clint Eastwood as "The Man with No Name" chews on a cigar, Marilyn Monroe's appearance tag was her low cut and tight fitting gown. Gary Burghoff as Radar in "MASH" carried a teddy-bear. These tags told more about the characters than pages of dialogue could have revealed.

Mannerism Tags

We all have mannerisms, even though we might not be aware of them. Giving your character the right mannerism makes him believable. You and I know the speaker who has to clear his throat before he starts his tirade, the woman who pouts in a childlike manner if something does not go her way, the salesman who executes a little bow before displaying another object for your approval, the hat-check girl who smiles her vacant, all-purpose smile. If you have seen "Ordinary People," you will always remember the slow, almost mechanical movements Mary Tyler Moore employed to care for her everyday things, such as napkins, tablecloths, laundry—all inanimate objects. This simple tag gave a frightening inside look into a woman whose emotions had withered to the point where she had to caress objects instead of living beings.

Expression Tags

Probably the most famous expression tag is Scarlett O'Hara's "Fiddledeedee." Expression tags will immediately categorize your characters as belonging to certain social and regional groups. But be careful, don't force actors to use trite expressions such as "I reckon" or "Mon dieux" to mark a character as an old farmer or a slightly effeminate French fashion designer. Listen to people. Get the melody of their speech, get the "way of putting things" peculiar to certain homogeneous groups. Expression tags worked beautifully in the first scenes of "The Deer Hunter." Each of the friends had a certain way of expressing himself that identified him individually and the group as a whole.

How to Reveal Your Characters

Keeping in mind that no screenwriter should permit any character to talk about himself at length, and that lengthy dialogues about the character's problems and goals should be avoided like black widow spiders, we still have the responsibility of letting our audience know all there is to know about our characters. Of course, as mentioned before, character should be revealed in action. Still, this is not always possible, nor is it always advisable. There are more subtle ways to achieve the same result. You have to probe into human behavior, and what controls human behavior. The deeper you probe, the more believable your character will become.

Contrast

By using contrasting characters—contrasting in looks, age, socioeconomic status, and behavior—you will be able to emphasize the characteristics of your main character. Take a look at Captain Holmes and his wife Karen in "From Here to Eternity" and you will see how perfectly those two characters are foils for each other. Holmes is stiff and indifferent while Karen is a woman of strong emotional existence.

Another excellent way of using contrast to reveal your main character is to contrast him with his environment. Again, in "From Here to Eternity" this technique is used to reveal Prewitt's character, a man unsuited to survive in the military environment of harsh discipline.

Conflict

Always put your characters into conflict situations. Without conflict there is no action, without action there is no audience interest, and without audience interest there is no sale. You see, it is a very simple formula. It does not matter whether you are writing a relationship, an action or a horror film. You must have conflict. Even in comedy, conflict situations are paramount. Just remember the famous "Pink Panther" films and the beloved "I Love Lucy" television shows.

Decision

Decision will force your character into action, and in deciding his course of action your character will reveal himself. Decisions are closely related to your character's sub-goals. As the sub-goals rise in intensity and seriousness, so must the decisions, until your character has reached the final and most crucial decision, his moment of truth. Usually the moment of truth is the end of your film. Nothing should be added once this point has been reached. The moment of truth comes for Leamas in "The Spy Who Came in From the Cold" as he steps off the Berlin wall towards his death.

Dialogue

You will find two different kinds of scenes in every screenplay, one where something happens visually—the action scene—and one given over to the spoken word—the dialogue scene. Each scene must reveal one element of story information. In addition, the dialogue scene must focus on the characters' relationships to one another. Of course, most action scenes have at least some dialogue, and often dialogue scenes feature some kind of action. Nevertheless, the information given to the audience is the main point of each scene.

Your dialogue scenes should never exceed three pages, and even this amount of dialogue should be looked upon with caution. As you write your dialogue scene keep Paddy Chayesky's advice in mind: "A play needs a good character, a good emotional relationship and a good crisis in that relationship." The moment you have digested this simple but sound advice, your dialogue will flow from your heart and not from your brain.

Good dialogue is not easy to write. Dialogue for film and television presents problems not encountered by the playwright who writes for the stage. One of the problems is the obvious brevity of screen versus stage dialogue. Where the playwright can have several paragraphs of dialogue, the screenwriter has to be content with a few sentences. Where the playwright uses sentences, the screenwriter uses a few words.

Another problem is posed by the fact that screen dialogue should not necessarily read well, but must fit into the character's mouth. Neophyte screenwriters are often too concerned with the "literary" look of their dialogue.

My advice is, don't bother with the look or screen-correctness of your dialogue during the first phases of your screenplay. Your first draft will be too long and over-written anyway. Forget about it. Don't worry. Let your characters say whatever is on their minds. Later on, as you revise, as plot and structure are set, then is the time to work on your dialogue. Dialogue is the "cherry on top of the sundae." It is the portion of your screenplay that needs polishing and rewriting until your dialogue has lost all of its elegance, and has turned into everyday speech. Dialogue must become an integral part of the character you have created. Ben Brady suggests: "Dialogue should not present the situation itself, but rather the situation as it is felt by the characters who are addressing it. Hence, if you truly know the emotional composition of your characters, it will find the right words to describe how it feels. This is derived from the amalgam of values and traits you have created."[*]

Keep the following suggestions in mind as you write and rewrite (and rewrite again) your dialogue:

- Keep your speeches short.
- If a speech is too long, simply let another character cut in.
- Keep your speeches lean.
- Characterize your speeches. Characters should *not* sound alike, but should be individualized. A New York doctor will sound different from the family doctor practicing in Little River. The waitress in "Mom's Diner" sounds different from the stockbroker's receptionist. A teenager in the 50s had a different vocabulary from the teenager of today.

Audience Identification

It is not enough that the audience passively watches your film. Your aim is to involve them *actively* with the story they see on the screen. You have worked hard to write *believable* characters, to raise your audience's emotions, to make them feel hope, fear, satisfaction or frustration. You have constructed your story in a way that will keep your audience in suspense, still, you may not have an interesting film. That is to say, a film that inspires the audience's active participation.

[*]Ben Brady "The Keys to Writing for Television and Film", Kendall Hunt Publishing Company, 1982.

During story conferences the term "interesting" always pops up. It is the cord around which writer, director and producer wind their expectations and demands. A film will only sell if it is interesting—if it hits some intangible emotional button in your audience. Let's face it, it is not the story that is interesting (and will sell tickets) or uninteresting, but it is the audience reaction to this story. If the spectators' *empathy* is involved then we speak about an interesting film. Empathy is the relation between story content and the life of the spectator. He must recognize, at least to some extent, his own hopes and fears, struggles and conflicts on the screen. This concept does not embrace his everyday life. There are few films which effectively portray Mr. Smith's fear of his boss, Mrs. Smith's struggle with the washing machine, and their continuous fight to keep up the monthly mortgage payments. No, this concept concerns his desires and his fears. These thoughts may be pointed towards universal goals like success, revenge, survival and reward.

Eugene Vale makes the following statement about the identification process: "Identification is caused by the desire to partake in other people's lives. This desire is particularly strong in people whose own lives are dull and empty... The motion picture audience consists to a large extent of people who are dissatisfied with their own lives."*

These people easily identify themselves with your characters on the screen, and it is your responsibility as a screenwriter to facilitate this empathy by creating characters that permit such identification. Primarily, your audience should feel empathy with the leading man and leading lady. No matter how idolized and larger than life your stars may seem, the spectator will identify himself with all the desirable attributes and the exciting situations exhibited on the screen. In this way the actor is a surrogate for the spectator's often subconscious wish-fulfillment. The spectrum of wish-fulfillment ranges from aggression to fear to hidden desires. Incidentally, this emotional bond created between star and spectator is one of the main reasons for creating stars.

The Special Niche of the Action and Horror Film

Keeping the aforementioned contentions about audience empathy in mind, it is not difficult to understand why action and horror films are the staple fare of the film industry. Fortunately for the low-budget film producer these films are within the perimeter of his production capabilities. We have seen "The Shining" and "Raiders of the Lost Ark"—both mega-bucks motion pictures featuring special effects way out of reach for the low-budget film producer. But fortunately it is still the story that counts.

Action films, as well as horror films, focus and play upon the audience's terror and need for survival. Remember these two basic human emotions as you construct your screenplay. Both film types follow basic ironclad rules. First, you should exploit a primitive fear, such as:

*Eugene Vale, "The Technique of Screenplay Writing ," The Universal Library, Grosset & Dunlap Publishers, New York, 1944.

Loss of Control
Claustrophobia
Fear of insects, snakes, etc.
Fear of ghosts, darkness and the unknown
Devils, demons, evil forces
Outer-space aliens
Children possessed by evil forces

After deciding upon and isolating a *specific fear,* you have pegged it to an identifiable evil behavior. There are only three basic evil behaviors:

- "Dr. Jekyll and Mr. Hyde" warns us that evil may exhibit itself in dual personalities and therefore may lurk everywhere. This fear makes us suspect our next door neighbor and our loved ones as well.
- "Frankenstein" deals with the danger of madness.
- "Dracula" explores the dualism of sexuality.

Of course, you may put these evil behaviors in all kinds of settings, past, present, or future.

Next, you have to make your story identifiable. You must find either a place that is familiar or strange to your audience. Your characters must be sympathetic—the audience must recognize their own fears and desires. The best way to fulfill this demand is to:

Put *everyday people* into *strange surroundings.*
Put *strange people* into *everyday surroundings.*

Once you have established the *positive* aspect of your story (the sunny beach, the friendly neighborhood), bring in the *negative* aspect of your story (the aliens, the killers). Vice versa, you establish the *strange* (negative) surroundings (the haunted house, the sinister town) and you bring in your *familiar* (positive) people (the young couple on their honeymoon, the group of vacationing teenagers).

Checklist for Your Screenplay

The old proverb says, "Watch out, if you cannot see the forest for the trees, you are in trouble." The same holds true for the screenplay. Once you have written your first draft, step back, let it simmer for a while, go on to something else. The possible mistakes which have occurred while you worked in the frenzy of creation are much more apparent after a few days of rest. As you have gained some distance between yourself and your screenplay check the following mistakes:

51

Identification
Lack of relation between story and life of spectators.
Lack of relation to audience interest at a given time.
Lack of sympathetic characters.
Lack of characters that an audience can identify with favorably.

Understandability
Lack of probability.
Insufficient information.
Exhausted formula.

Structure
No discernable main goal.
No countergoal.
Either the main goal or the countergoal is too weak.
The main goal and countergoal are being introduced too late.
Lack of graduation.
Uneven graduation.
No switches at conclusion of each act.
Sub-goals are not overlapping.
Choppiness because sequence of scenes does not follow interest.

Suspense
Unequal chances of success.
Failure to expose difficulty.
Lack of surprise.
Lack of anticipation.
Failure to satisfy or frustrate sub-intention.
Failure to focus counter-intention upon the same goal.

Characterization
Vague or improbable traits.
Lack of sufficient and interesting tags.
No contrast in characters.
Stilted dialogue.
Dialogue is wrong for the character.
Character is not permitted to develop his characterization by "action."
Uninteresting environment.

Chapter Five

The Creative Team

Once the script has been written it takes the combined efforts of the director, cinematographer, lighting director and art director to give the film its shape and form. That is to say, to bring it to a point of fulfillment where art, technique and insight interact. The film will be affected by the way your creative team defines reality, both internal and external. Gertrude Stein summed up this thought in her observation that "the composition in which we live makes the art in which we see and hear."

We can say that the art of the feature film is the true artistic expression of the 20th century. The film most effectively—and at times disturbingly—mirrors our sense of identity. Today's film is most effectively approached as a dramatic art combining the contradictory areas of technique, psychology and individual expression. Strangely enough, the "individual expression" rests in the hands and minds of a group of people who will express their artistic visions through a purely technological medium.

Let's take a closer look at these purveyors of the motion picture's unique qualities.

The Director

The director dramatizes the film's ideas and concept. He gives life to the script by creating concrete images such as things, places and people. He is the one who immerses the audience in the literal actuality of what is happening on screen. Using the techniques of composition, direction and action, he establishes a pattern of relationship between the audience and the action on screen. He is the one who decides on which details to select, what statement to make, what evaluations to either signify or obscure. In this respect he has to face the awesome responsibility that film, being a mass medium, will effect and even change many lives. On a more mundane level, his task is to have objects—like houses, landscapes, neighborhoods, and so on—interact with events and human relationships. Only the film is able to convey the meaning of environment by using it as a dramatic statement. The setting must play an integral part in the development of theme and human relationships.

Today's film director has to deal with a totality of expression unknown to any other artist. Given the freedom of the editing process, he can manipulate reality to affect the responses of the audience in a way unknown before the advent of the film, while the camera focuses audience attention at precisely the spot he has selected. He has the power to change the perspective from which we view things, events, and emotions.

Even though two basic techniques have emerged during the past years, each director has his own way of directing a film. Some directors go for shorter and more diverse scenes. They put their emphasis on movement, which tends to minimize the verbal statement. Others go for slow, almost epic movements involving all our senses. Directors like Fellini and Bergman make us "see" in the truest sense of the word.

Finding the "Right" Director

Directors emerge from all fields of the motion picture industry. Most likely they are experts in such diversified fields as:

Editing
Producing
Writing
Acting
Cinematography

Realizing that the director is the true creator of the film, sooner or later everyone working in the above listed areas experiences an incurable itch to try his hand at directing. "Anyway," they argue, "I am an expert in my own niche. I have worked on many films. I have watched many directors, and I bet that I can do their job just as well, if not better."

You, being a new producer trying to get your small, low-budget film off the ground, are likely to be forced into considering a first time director who has demonstrated his effectiveness in one of these areas, but is a novice in the director's chair. Let's take a look at all these new directors auditioning for you, and let's quickly decide who might be the best candidate for the job. At this point you may do well to forget the terrific demo reel each one presents you with. A demo reel can be a misleading little time bomb. You will never discover which elements have "grown in your candidate's garden" and which may be attributed to the expertise of the lighting director and the cinematographer. Push the demo reel aside for the time being, and instead concentrate on your candidate's background. Experience has taught me to rate first time directors (based on a scale from one to ten) as follows:

Editors	8-10
Cinematographers	5-7
Actors	3-7
Producers	3-5
Writers	1-3

Please remember, we speak about "first time directors." Each and every one of the fields listed has produced creative and knowledgeable directors—once they had made their initial mistakes. You, however, cannot afford to serve as mentor, and the film you are producing cannot serve as a training ground for any new director. You have to make certain that the talent you hire will serve best as the captain of your cinematographic ship. Now is the time to discuss the pros and cons of each candidate.

Editor

Without any doubt, Max the editor is your best bet. You can hardly go wrong entrusting a skilled and creative editor with the task of directing your film. He knows how the film will go together. As he dissects the script into various camera set-ups, he automatically envisions the way he will cut the finished product. Besides, he knows about:

Continuity
Screen direction
Matching action in cuts
Transitions

You will never lose any time while he and the cinematographer argue about the flow of direction in a certain scene. Max knows which way the actors have to move. After all, he has edited a great number of films. He will never waste any time or film shooting the expensive, traditional way of shooting a master shot, medium shot, reversals and close-ups. No, Max will "edit in the camera," a term dear to the heart of every low-budget film producer. Max will only shoot the shots important to the film. As he sets up his shot list, he already is editing the film in his mind.

Yet, there is another side to Max. Most likely he is not well versed in the area of acting. His choice of characters and types will reflect type-casting as he goes out for the true and proven, namely actors who represent easily recognizable types, know their lines and are able to hit marks. Most likely, Max will leave them to their own devices, giving only the barest hints of directorial advice. If he is dealing with creative and skilled actors, he has it made. The actors sensing their creative freedom, will "run with the film," they will mold and sculpt their characters. If Max is lucky enough to work with secure actors, one will see truly creative performances. But, the actors must be mature enough to appreciate the benefits of ensemble work. No one should try to overshadow the other.

At other times, if he is too content with good "types" but poor actors, Max ends up with either uninspired, wooden or uneven performances, wondering what went wrong.

Cinematographer

Steve the cinematographer, like Max, knows all the basic rules of directing. Continuity and screen direction will never present any problems to him. Steve will give you gorgeous compositions. The pictures you see on the screen are works of art. He is the one who gives you the mood of your film, the creator of all those eerie shadows creeping down the stairs in your haunted house, the one who makes a single leaf in the upper left hand corner of your frame come alive. Steve gives your film class.

But he takes his own sweet time working on his masterpiece. No one can hurry him. Blissfully he forgets about the shooting script while he "creates." More than likely, Steve is not greatly concerned about the actors entrusted to him. After all, can any human anguish compete with the fury of the Niagara Falls he tries to capture? The pictorial statement comes first with Steve, and therefore, while he has an excellent eye for faces and character types, he might insist on hiring actors unsuited as far as talent is concerned.

If you do not mind going over your schedule, for say two or three days, and if the pictorial element either outweighs or balances the emotional statement you wish to make, then Steve is your man. Same as Max, he needs to be supported by creative and independent actors. If everything falls in place, and if you can afford to go slightly overboard on your budget, then Steve will bring in a work of art.

Actor

Ralph, the actor, is at his best directing a film of high emotional content and dealing with intricate human relationships. He orchestrates his actors like so many instruments in an symphony. Angrily he will push aside all suggestions about type casting, and will instead search for the actor who is precisely right. He will insist on doing his own casting, and will spend infinite care on even the smallest part to be cast. The actors he selects are not only "right" they are knowledgeable actors of stature, well versed in all aspects of film acting. You, the producer, will never lose any time while your leading lady stumbles over her feet and forgets her lines.

Ralph will be a dictator with your actors, demanding from each the same dedication he displays. He will not go for "creative outbursts," but forces all of his actors to comply with his vision of how the role should be portrayed. It is true, many actors make exciting directors if they deal with a film based on verbal statements.

Unfortunately Ralph's expertise regarding the technical aspects of his task—such as camera moves, continuity and screen direction—are at best vague. Even an actor who has performed in many film and television shows, and is familiar with the process, still lacks the training that both the editor and the cinematographer possess.

Much time will be lost and some film may be wasted as Ralph figures out the purely technical aspects of his job. Yet, if you consider focusing your film upon relationships rather than action or pictorial statement, then you will fare well with Ralph. Ralph should realize he has to depend on a strong cinematographer. He needs many meetings with the director of cinematography. All camera set-ups and moves have to be worked out in advance and in concert. No one should have any surprises up his sleeve once the camera starts rolling, therefore he should be asked to submit a storyboard.

Ralph will bring in an excellent film if he and the director of cinematography work as a team. You as the producer should not permit any flare-ups of ego or imagined supremacy by either party. If the ugly monster of ego raises his head on your shoot, you will go dangerously over budget. In any event, you will be saddled with a film that presents its share of editing problems.

Producer

Producers are human like everyone else. They get sick and tired seeing everyone else happily swimming in the sea of creativity while they have to sweat over books and budgets. It irks them to no end to nurture a project, to worry over financing, often to spend sixteen hours a day doing unrewarding work, only to have to turn their brainchild over to someone else once the first day of principal photography starts. Yes, they want to have their day too. Anthony, the producer, wants to partake in applause and recognition. He is tired of paying bills and listening to peoples' gripes. Anthony wants to direct.

Unfortunately, Anthony should think twice before he hires himself for his new picture. It is true, he has hired directors and cinematographers and editors before—he knows about their craft. And this is the point of departure: he knows *about* their craft, but he has not *learned* their craft. The same holds true for the actors he has to hire. He knows what he wants, but lacks the knowledge about what makes their art, and personality, exciting. Anthony, without any doubt, will stick to each day's shooting list as if his life depended on it. Each added take will gnaw on his conscience like the legendary serpent. He will bring in his film on time and on budget *if* he surrounds himself with knowledgeable people, *if* he will listen to their advice, *if* he is willing to turn over the producer's duties (and clout) to someone else. While he directs his first movie, he should not worry about all the many things he is used to worrying about.

One word of advice, if you are producing your first film, forget about directing it. Both jobs are too demanding to be tackled simultaneously.

Writer

Bill, the writer, is low man on the totem pole when it comes to directing his own script. This statement seems an anachronism. I must agree, no one knows the script better than the writer. He has created it. The story, the plot, even the characters are his own. Of all people he ought to be the most suited for the task of directing.

The truth of the matter is that Bill is so close to his own script that as director he might insist on set-ups and takes that are unnecessary for the overall concept of the film. Besides, like the producer and actor, he lacks the required technical knowledge in the areas of directing, as well as acting. Once Bill the writer has gained experience and insight, his chances of bringing in a good film will be better. At least he will interpret his script as it was written, without being subjected to some of the inane changes that producers and directors often demand.

Assistant Director

Next to the editor, Fred your assistant director is your best choice. He has been in the trenches, he knows what directing is all about. If he has worked for some of the very best directors, so much so better.

Assessing The Director's Demo Reel

Once you have gotten some insight into your prospective director's background, and you have narrowed down your choice to two or three possibilities, you are ready to look at demo reels.* All artistic and aesthetic considerations aside, you should evaluate the tape for its technical expertise and knowhow only. You will base your judgment about the director's abilities upon the following:

Matching of action in shots
Screen direction
Point of vitality in each scene
Knowledge of anticipation
Handling of suspense

Matching of Action in Shots

One of your major considerations is to determine how well the director has matched the action happening at the end of one shot with the continuation of that action at the beginning of the next shot. Only if the director has shot an overlap will both actions match. Each action has to move smoothly to its designated point. There should not be any abrupt changes. For instance:

MEDIUM SHOT: Girl rising from chair—beginning of movement
CAMERA PULLS BACK
TO FULL SHOT: Girl continues to rise
DOLLY SHOT: Girl walks off screen camera left

Matching of action shots is highly important for all fight and chase scenes. Since there is always the danger of some choppiness in a fight scene, the skilled director will shoot some coverage. Close-ups of faces, hands or feet smooth out any unevenness. Still he will be careful that the position of the point of action matches from shot to shot.

Screen Direction

Maintaining a consistent screen direction for any moving object in a series of shots is your next point for observation. Controlling the direction of motion on the screen is one of the basic requirements of the skilled director.

---

* A demo reel is a 3/4-inch tape showing excerpts of the director's work.

Take a look at the drawing, and you will see the BLACK CAR is always to the screen RIGHT, while the WHITE CAR chasing it is always to the screen LEFT. The SAME DIRECTION must be maintained or the audience will become confused. If the director wishes to CHANGE SCREEN DIRECTION, he must insert a NEUTRAL SHOT. In other words, he must shoot a FRONTAL VIEW of the BLACK CAR. Only then he will be able to change, so that in the next sequence the BLACK CAR will be Screen LEFT and the WHITE CAR screen RIGHT.

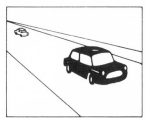  

The same holds true in REVERSAL SHOTS. Filming a conversation between two people, the actor established on screen LEFT remains there while the actor established on screen RIGHT maintains his position throughout the scene.

Another aspect of screen direction pertains to the correct use of close-ups after an establishing medium shot. Here the director must be aware that the close-up look must match the one in the medium shot. To save time and film, the knowledgeable director will shoot the beginning and the conclusion of a dialogue first in a medium shot, and then will move in to the close-ups. Care should be taken that the close-ups are shot with opposing looks. These looks must be consistent with the medium shot. Depending on their height, one actor might look below the lens while his partner looks above the lens. The director must concern himself with camera height, besides screen direction, during the shooting of any close-up. The basic rule is: the higher actor looks below the lens, the lower actor looks above the lens.

Probably the most effective way of judging a director's basic knowledge is his use of directional transition—that is, the smooth flow from full shot to close-up or vice versa. Such a transition should not call any undue attention to itself. The director should always supply the editor with a transitional medium shot. The following sequence would not cut well:

FULL SHOT: Party scene—people talking and milling around
CLOSE-UP: Millie and Jim dancing

Yet, with the transitional medium shot, the scene will look decidedly different:

FULL SHOT: Party scene—people talking and milling around

MEDIUM SHOT: A group of people dancing, among them Millie and Jim

CAMERA MOVES IN
TO CLOSE-UP ON: Millie and Jim dancing

Point of Vitality in Each Scene

Writing his shooting script, the director should put himself in the place of the audience viewing the picture. In this respect the *point of vitality* is of prime importance. Often, at the beginning of a scene there is some wasted time, and after the highpoint the scene meanders to its end. True, much of the waste can (and will) be edited out. But film that does not serve its purpose is an expense the low-budget film producer cannot permit. The director must develop the core of the action sufficiently but economically, recognizing the point of vitality as its apex.

Each scene must have its beginning, its high point (or point of vitality) and its end. The entire scene must be geared to the apex. All deadwood has to be avoided.

Judging the Director's Visual Image

The unifying perspective of the director's attitude—his style—is expressed in the accumulation of many separate elements. His manner of handling dramatic action in a visual way demonstrates itself most effectively in:

The composition of the individual shot.
The symbolism of the individual shot.

Now is the time to put the director's demo reel aside and to concentrate on his films. Only if you view a completed film will you be able to assess whether or not the director's style is right for the picture you envision. Basically we speak about three different styles:

Epic Style
Realistic Style
Expressive Style

Composition of the Individual Shot

In the composition of his shots the director relates aesthetic qualities to his dramatic statement. That is to say, he captures the mood of the moment and the emotional state of the characters on the screen. In any case, the composition of the shot does not refer as much to the shape and color masses on the screen as it does to the psychological statement these structures make. Unlike the composition of a painting or photograph, the composition of a shot is dynamic. In this respect, the composition of a shot should tell the mood of the moment immediately, and without the encumbrance of spoken words.

Picture two lovers walking next to each other. In the first shot they walk hand in hand on the beach. The immenseness of the surf behind them, the cloudless blue sky and the expanse of sandy beach will give the audience a feeling of freedom and happiness. By the same token, the audience will become subconsciously aware of the truth that we human beings are just unimportant specks in the universe. Our own happiness or sorrows are unimportant in the face of nature.

In the second shot the lovers are separated by prison bars. The horizontal shape of the bars alone give the composition its tightness. Subconsciously again, the audience will experience a feeling of suffocation and helplessness. It is the same feeling of helplessness that the two lovers on screen are likely to feel. If the scene is set up in a tight medium shot, then this feeling of frustration will be heightened. While the lovers were of secondary importance in the first shot, they now have achieved supremacy. Their emotions and actions are far more interesting than the environment surrounding them.

The Symbolism of the Individual Shot

Symbols for emotions and states of mind have become cliche in many cases. We all have witnessed ad nauseam the friend pacing restlessly up and down the hospital corridor while the clock on the wall ticks away time. Symbols, in order to be effective, should be a part of the dramatic action, and must be an integral part of the scene. The audience should never become intellectually aware of the function of the symbol used. Because of the selectiveness of the camera, the film gives heightened significance to everyday objects. Some directors very effectively use Fellini's method of repetition and variation of one and the same symbol all through the film. In "Lilith," Robert Rossen uses variations of bars and wire fences to symbolize the psychological imprisonment of his characters.

61

Elia Kazan's "On the Waterfront" places the climactic scene between Terry and his brother Charley in a cab. The turned back of the cab driver and the street lights flashing by outside both symbolize Terry's plight, as the cab will probably take him to his death.

The use of composition and symbolism is open to everyone, even the director working on a small, low-budget film. These two integral functions of the film as an art form, do not cost more money, do not take any more time, but demand some creativity and insight. More than once has a sensitive director turned a run-of-the-mill, low-budget feature into a small miracle of art because he did his homework on those two counts.

Directing Styles

Whether or not your prospective director admits to it, he does have a certain way of doing it, a "handwriting"—in short, a style of his own.

Epic Style

Looking at Francis Coppola's "The Godfather" and Michael Cimino's "The Deer Hunter" we see outstanding examples of the epic style of cinematographic expression. True, the low-budget film cannot even dream to tackle this style. Still, some low-budget film directors have a distinct leaning to the epic format, and bring in outstanding results on comparatively small budgets.

The epic film is constructed by combining the elements of individual conflict into larger blocks of struggle. The synthesis of the epic film is larger than life in both its intensity and its display of masses of people and impressive settings. In this respect many of the low-budget Westerns so popular in the 40s and 50s achieved a truly epic style.

Realistic Style

Realism, the depiction of a "slice of life," is the prevalent style for film. Taking for granted Suzanne Langer's opinion that "art is a matter of forms symbolic of human feeling," we will be able to observe the ever changing shift of our mores and ways of thinking simply by watching contemporary movies.

The people, their actions and emotions are the center of each and every realistic film. This film style accurately traces everyday reality, drawing the audience into an illusion of reality unsurpassed by any art form. This style places strong emphasis on social setting and social custom, presenting these details with accuracy. Plot and storyline following a psychological motive and reaction concept provide a clear context in which the characters move from cause to effect. The social statement is a strong factor in the realistic film, and many griping, realistic films, such as John Ford's "The Grapes of Wrath," construct a convincing social message.

The message might deal with the interaction between the individual and his environment, the struggle of the individual with himself, and the need for communal affirmation. The realistic film may be sympathetic or accusative with the problems extolled, but it always shows life as it is. Generally a monochromatic mood prevails in this type of picture, and the simplicity and, at times, awkwardness of the low-budget film lends itself well to the matter-of-factness of this style.

Expressive Style

Shortly after World War II, notably with DeSica's "Bicycle Thief" a new style emerged. Filmmakers began to structure their pictures with less plot, but emphasized the revelation of the human spirit. Their films did not move from cause to effect anymore, but found their reverberation in the echoes of the same theme. This "remaining in the same spot" was visible on the pictorial as well as emotional level of their films. The best exponent of this style was Roberto Rossellini. Using distorted perspective, off-center composition and lingering close-ups, he forced the audience into introspection.

Basically, the expressive style goes beyond the surface of the clearly visible. It builds a comprehensive structure of its individual sense of reality. This reality is neither accurate nor static, but is in constant flux, giving a subjective interpretation of the filmmaker's point of view. The expressive style examines the psychological reality of knowledge, perception and comprehension, moving it to man's inner world of ambiguity. It breaks with the habitual notions of identity, motivation and choice.

Many expressive style films borrow heavily on Brechtian devices. The structure is loose and very flexible, the stress more on psychological resolution than on plot resolution. One finds undynamic interchanges, and overall, a kind of dislocating technique emerges into a highly interesting mix of tones within each single scene.

Brecht stressed "the vital multiplicity, the innumerable shadings, the all moving unrest of contradictions" in all of his stage plays. The same holds true for the expressive style film. True, the low-budget filmmaker cannot afford to build his films upon a purely subjective structure. After all, his "slice of life"—horror and action films—must be understood by a wide audience. He sells to the mass media, not a few art gourmets. Still, he should study the techniques of the expressive film. Snatches here and there will improve his films immensely, making them more interesting and more viable.

The Director's Duties

Once the script has been approved, the director should be the first one of the creative team involved in pre-production. From now on he will share responsibilities with the producer in the following areas:

Shooting script
Casting and rehearsals
Location hunt
Decision on hiring art director and director of photography

Shooting Script

It is the director's responsibility to dissect the script, first into scenes which are the basis of the final budget, and then into individual shot lists. At times he has to prove his intended shot list with an accompanying storyboard.*

It is not his duty to rewrite the script. He may make a suggestion here or there, but it is entirely up to the producer to approve or disapprove any changes. Unfortunately, many producers, contending that the director is "the truly creative force" on any picture, permit an aggressive director to rework the script to his liking. They disregard the fact that the director is only creative as far as the *interpretation* of the script is concerned. Most likely his skill pertains to his directorial duties only, not to writing. The producer already paid a writer for his services. If there are any doubts about the script, it is the writer's duty to rewrite. The writer is far more knowledgeable about plot line and characterization than the producer and director combined.

The first two weeks of a director's residence on a film usually tells whether he will be cooperative, or whether he will throw his weight around. Since the script is likely to give cause for some contention, the wise producer establishes early on who runs the show.

Casting

Generally, the producer is responsible for the "star names." The producer has been informed by the distributor as to who is acceptable, and the director should not interfere with choices of his own. As far as the rest of the cast is concerned, casting falls within the director's area of responsibility. Still, on many low-budget, small films the producer has already assembled a cast by the time the director has been hired. Even though the director will try to make the best of the cast handed to him (in most cases, at least), he should not refrain from voicing his objections, if one or the other actor is unsuited type-wise or talent-wise.

Location Hunt

The days spent "location hunting" are the most enjoyable during any production. There is an air of excitement, a feeling that a story finally becomes a reality as one looks for the actual places and settings for the film. It is very helpful if the director of photography and the art director have a word in the final decision. At times, a room or an alley does not lend itself as well to the prospective scene as the director and producer had envisioned. The director of photography knows how long it will take to set up lighting. He knows whether or not the camera set-ups

* A story board shows each shot in a number of continuous drawings.

64

that the director suggests are possible. The art director can determine what kind of "dressing" each set will require. The decision on location should be made in concert with these various key people.

At this point everyone should defer to the producer's final decision. After all, he is the one who has to justify the cost of the location, deciding whether or not it is in accordance with his budget. Many a time he has to decline a terrific location, simply because it requires to much dressing, or does not fit within the budget, production time, or transportation limitations. In conclusion, make it very clear to the director that while he is in charge of the *creative directorial* element of your film, you still have the final word on everything concerning the production. Do not permit him to:

- Hire any actor or crew member without your approval.
- Contract for any location, sets, props, vehicles, etc. without your approval.
- Make payments (over $50) without your approval.

Director of Photography

Hiring a director of photography is not an easy task. The producer may do well to listen to the director's advice and select a person with whom the director has worked before. In any event, the director and cinematographer should be able to communicate well with each other, and should be familiar with their respective styles and manner of working. It is essential to the smooth flow of each production day that director and cinematographer are a team. No matter how enthusiastically your director speaks about a cinematographer, it is the producer's responsibility to assess the director of photography's demo reel. You will look for the following:

Balance
Symmetry
Framing
Juxtaposition
Framing of close-ups
Staging
Picturization

Looking at cartoons in newspapers will teach you the basic requirements of good composition. The well drawn cartoon tells a great deal concerning framing and staging. Learn how to look at the cinematographer's demo reel from this design point of view.

Balance
Objects and people must be arranged within a frame so that they balance properly. This means that one shot should not outweigh the next

shot in mass and color. All distinctly horizontal or vertical lines should be placed slightly beyond the center.

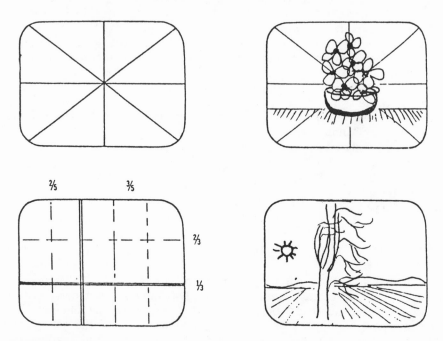

Symmetry

Placing an object (or person) exactly in the middle of your screen is not very exciting. If you want to emphasize a single object you may do well to place it slightly to the side. The same applies to a crowd or party scene. Do not place your lead actors symmetrically or the scene will look stagnant no matter how lively the extras in the background move about.

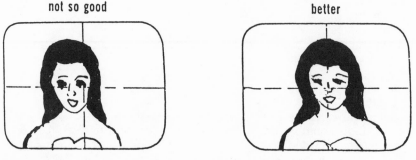

Framing

Close-ups and tight medium shots *should* place the actor symmetrically in the middle of the frame. Be aware that the viewer should not be given a chance to be distracted by unnecessary elements.

If the actor looks in a direction left or right of the camera, leave some space in the direction he is looking, although he should not touch the edge of the screen with either nose or head.

If you wish to frame the actor close to the edge of the screen, then *something must take place behind him.*

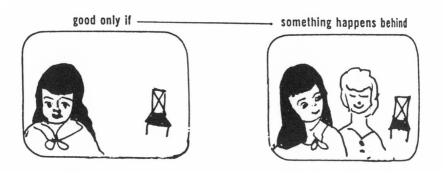

Extremely high or low angle shots should be avoided unless you wish to make a specific statement. A high angle shot suggests humbleness, a low angle shot makes a person huge and often brutal looking.

high camera position:
looking down

low camera position:
looking up

Juxtaposition

Watch for the strange looking juxtaposition of performers and props. Houses should not grow on your lead man's shoulder, and your leading lady doesn't look attractive with a tree sprouting from her head.

bad

bad

Framing of Close-Ups

In an extreme close-up (XCU) it is better to cut the upper rather than the lower part of the head.

bad

better

Staging

Staging a "two shot" in front of the camera is not easy. If you stage your actors side by side you will often get unflattering profiles. A profile shot is usually ineffective. Only the frontal view of a face will give the actor the opportunity to play the entire range of his emotions. For these reasons, downstage-upstage positioning is usually better than lateral positioning. The "star," or more important actor, should always face the camera—that is, he should be placed downstage.

In the popular "over the shoulder" shot you will have to be aware of the "gray line" rule. Both camera set-ups should be on one side, or the actors will seem to jump from side to side. That is, the cameras should be positioned on the same side of the actor. The illustration shows a gray area. Placing the camera there will cause a difficult cut during editing.

Showing an Actor at a Window

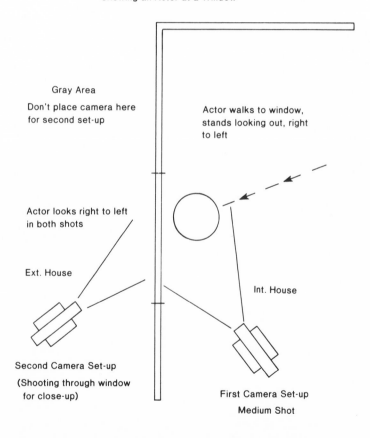

Gray Area

Don't place camera here
for second set-up

Actor walks to window,
stands looking out, right
to left

Actor looks right to left
in both shots

Ext. House

Int. House

Second Camera Set-up

(Shooting through window
for close-up)

First Camera Set-up

Medium Shot

To maintain consistent direction of looks, both camera set-ups should
be from same side of actor. Placing camera for second set-up in the gray
area will cause an uncomfortable cut when two pieces of film are spliced
together.

Picturization

In film language, picturization refers to the succession of shots. Picturization needs movement. Remember, film is moving pictures. It consists of:

The movement in front of camera.
The movement of the camera.
The movement achieved by adding picture to picture.

Dolly and *pan* change the picture smoothly, and *cut, dissolve*, and *fade* will change the picture abruptly. We can divide picturization into three categories:

Primary movement: the movement in front of the camera (actors or events).
Secondary movement: the movement of the camera itself.
Tertiary movement: the succession of pictures achieved in the editing process.

Primary Movement: Movement toward or away from the camera is much more interesting than any lateral movement. If it is artistically sound, you will achieve a stronger effect by having your actor walk towards or away from the camera. During lateral movement you must lead your actor, not trail him.

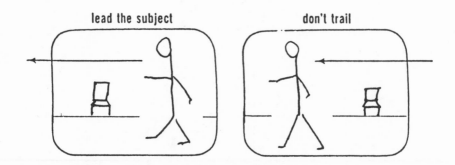

Secondary Movement: Secondary movement is valid as soon as it helps to tell the story, or to make a statement. If used for quasi "artistic" purposes, it gives a self-conscious effect.

Pan: The reason for panning is to follow the action. Do not permit too much dead space. Your panning should be as fast as the objects you have to follow.

Tilt: You may tilt to follow action or to create a dramatic effect. You can create suspense by slowly tilting up to Mother Superior's stern face.

Dolly: A dolly-in will gradually enlarge an object on the screen. A dolly-back has the opposite effect. Usually you go from the general to the specific, or the specific to the general. Depending on the dolly speed, you will be able to make strong or subtle points.

Zoom: A zoom is often used instead of a dolly shot. We all are familiar with the "shock zoom" of the horror film, which is used to emphasize something quickly and dramatically. If used with care, the zoom can be very effective. You may zoom in or zoom back.

Truck: A truck shot is a lateral movement of the camera. You may use a truck shot to follow lateral action, or you may truck along stationary objects. A truck shot looks very impressive, as the objects in the foreground move slowly past the screen, while the background objects remain stationary. The truck shot is one of the standard devices of the epic film.

The knowledgeable cinematographer will design the scene to be filmed into a series of overall shots of activity. Often he has to tell a story in terms of action as well as feeling. Where the camera is placed in relation to action can make the difference between a shot expressing the writer's and director's intention fully or halfheartedly. The camera should be placed at such an angle as to catch the true importance of what is happening. Orchestrating motions into visual experiences and perceptions is the cinematographer's task.

Director of Lighting

In color films, lighting is extremely important. The direction of lighting affects the audience indirectly through its effect on the colors used. Lighting, like color, can be functional and expressive at the same time. The skilled lighting director—an artist in his own right—will be able to create magic with but the essentials of lighting equipment. He knows the direction of the lighting plot established by the key light, the degree of diffusion or the intensity required for the individual scenes. The tone established by lighting sets the emotional mood of the film. Dark lighting is associated with somber or mysterious moods, bright lighting with joy and happiness. Contrasts in the lighting itself is an important factor in intensifying the dramatic situation.

Lighting, the same as with details of color, can carry symbolic associations. Color has now become integrated with the dramatic context, and is one of the most vital expressive conventions of the contemporary film. Lighting and color are used to emphasize the dramatic statement. For years color was primarily used to enhance the look of epic spectacles. But the style has changed. In today's cinema we employ color to suggest tone and the environment of the location. Color and light are now integral parts of the story to be told. By blurring, filtering, or misting the various hues, the lighting director externally visualizes the emotional core of the scene.

Art Director

The ideal art director for the low-budget film is not only an artist in his field, but he knows about all kinds of environments, styles and times. He is a never ending worker, has at least some knowledge of carpentry, and is a wizard in the art of creating props and set pieces out of thin air. Additionally, he should have the artist's eye for creating a "picture" out of any ordinary setting. He should know about depth staging for the desired three dimensional effect required for film.

He should be aware that most directors prefer to shoot on an "angle," that is, they dislike the confinement of straight walls. Unfortunately, most locations are just that—four straight walls. The art director should be ready to create some framing. He will make good use of the characteristics of the camera lens (short lens exaggerating relative size, long lens reducing the feeling of depth) as he sets up his props. In setting up a depth-staged set, he will show some prominent foreground piece which makes the other objects seem smaller. He also will be aware that the set pieces have to balance with the action or the actors. Unless so desired, neither props nor set pieces should draw attention to themselves and away from the actors.

The producer cannot assess every penny which has to be spent on set construction, construction of props, props and related purchases. It is human nature to be just a little less careful with someone else's money, and it is easy for even the most conscientious and honest art director to go a little overboard once in a while—to buy an item just a trifle more expensive than necessary. But in a low-budget film, each and every dollar spent counts.

I found it advantageous to supply the art director with a fixed sum, the so called "Art Director's Budget." This sum, along with his salary is usually paid in three installments:

During pre-production.
Beginning of principal photography.
Completion of principal photography.

I always explain to the art director that the allocated money is all he can spend. There won't be any more funds for his department. I also let him know that any amount he saves constitutes a little bonus for him, providing that the sets and props meet with my approval.

Chapter Six

The Casting Process

How to Find Actors

Actors are the lifeblood of each and every film in production. Casting directors, producers and directors spend much time looking for the "right" actor, the right person, the right type, the right age group. But finding this right and exciting actor is like looking for the proverbial needle in the haystack. Yes, there is an abundance of actors. It is true, the supply by far outweighs the demand. Still, there is a relatively small number of talented and skilled people in this profession. The acting profession is the only one people try to enter without at least some training or knowledge. As actors knock on your door, you'll have to learn to separate the winners from the losers. You, the producer, and the director will spend many days interviewing and reading actors until you have finally discovered the ones perfect to breathe the breath of life into the characters of your script.

If you are signatory to SAG (Screen Actor's Guild), if you are doing a "union" film, you will face no difficulties having agents submit their clients. It is true, SAG membership does not make a skilled actor. There are many untalented members of this coveted union, and there are numerous excellent actors who have not yet had the opportunity of joining SAG. Still, hiring a union actor gives you at least some assurance that he will be able to read his lines and hit his marks. It is very difficult to join SAG. Unfortunately, it is neither the prospective member's talent or training that will get him into the union, but only the fact that he was able to garner three days work on a union feature film or television show (extra work will not get the actor into SAG, he must speak lines). For this reason, membership in any union is no guarantee of the actor's knowledge about acting in general, and motion picture acting in particular. Regardless of the great number of actors available, there are comparatively few good ones. The non-union low-budget producer has his work cut out for him. He will spend many hours going through stacks of pictures and resumes, and he will spend days reading actors. Many low-budget film producers simply cannot afford the fees demanded by the union, and it is impossible for them to agree to the working hours the union requires. The day on a low-budget shoot is ten hours or more.

It is more than likely that the producer in pre-production of a low-budget film will advertise in one of the trades—"Drama-Logue" and "Casting Call" in Hollywood and "Back Stage" in New York. Emotionally and physically he must be ready for an avalanche. Pictures and resumes will be everywhere—on the floor, on the furniture, on the walls—and still they come in. The mail carrier reminds you gently of the up-coming holidays, he subtly suggests that he is ready for a nice little reward as he hands you another fifty envelopes. Honestly, you will have to go through over a thousand pictures during the two to three weeks after your ad appears. Many of the pictures will end up in your waste basket. Throwing a picture out is a difficult task for most producers. They know how actors sacrifice for these glossies and composites, how much hope accompanied the mailed eight by tens.* Still, there are so many actors who would be better off in any other occupation.

You will narrow the field somewhat by asking several mailing services to send pictures of their clients. These mailing services regularly send the pictures of their clients to production companies. You may even request them to send certain types of actors. Unfortunately, the actor's employing mailing services are usually SAG members, and therefore out of your reach.

Pictures

Obviously you cannot interview every actor who submitted his picture. Unless you bring some method to the madness of the casting process, the time spent on getting your cast together will take up too much space within the time allotment of your pre-production schedule. I usually start casting about three months before the start of principal photography. I give myself eight weeks to find my cast, then I turn the actors over to the director for rehearsal. I do not issue contracts at this point. In case the director decides after a week that an actor has to be replaced, I still have some time to look for a suitable actor. If you are producing a union shoot you'll have to pay the actor's entire contractual salary. On a non-union shoot, you pay for rehearsal time only.

Going through the submitted pictures (after you fixed yourself a fortifying cup of coffee), you'll sort them out into three groups:

Suitable as far as type is concerned.
Suitable as far as age group is concerned.
Unsuitable on both counts, but otherwise interesting.
   (At times this group turns out to be extremely useful, as it turns you away from the "beaten path" and offers some interesting casting choices.)

The last group—the "hopeless" ones—will be filed in file thirteen, the wastepaper basket, no matter how much this cruel action will hurt you. Do not read the resumes during this process of casting, but concentrate on the *look* of the actors. Unless you are producing a highly realistic slice of life film, you will be forced to *typecast* at least the minor roles.

Typecasting seeks the *look* of an actor that the audience can identify with immediately. Typecasting works on the audience's subconscious mind. If an actor looks like the audience thinks a police officer, an

*Glossy photographs the actors submit with their resume.

74

attorney, or a teacher should look, then the actor is *type*. Most casting directors will cast a meek looking man for the role of an accountant, even though their own accountant is over six feet tall, and used to be a linebacker for the UCLA football team. For the run-of-the-mill low-budget horror or action film, they will search for handsome young men and gorgeous young girls—in short, actors and actresses the audience will admire, and hopefully fall in love with. All motion pictures aim to work on the viewer's empathy. It does not matter whether the film tries to raise social conscience, or whether it is meant to entertain.

Unknown to himself, the viewer will establish a relationship with the hero or heroine on the screen—he will put himself into the actor's shoes. If a film works, the audience will participate with the events on the screen as if these were happening to themselves.

Going through the actor's eight by tens you should select about four to five candidates for each minor part to be filled.

Resume

Once you have found the "right types" to portray the characters in your story, your next consideration should be the resume attached to each picture. Many casting directors claim that the resume is more important than the picture. The basic function of the resume is to inform any prospective employer about the actor's experience. At times, the resume tells more about an actor than he wishes to be known. If it flutters on your desk, showing traces of coffee stains, if it regales you with misspelled words, if the typing is careless, you may bet your last dollar, that the actor is as careless about his work as he is about his resume. The resume that is to the point, neatly typed and neatly reproduced points to an actor who most likely will be efficient, who will know his lines and arrive on the set promptly.

Assume you are casting the role of a priest. It is a small part, requiring about two days of shooting, but the role is important to plot development and should be cast with an impressive actor. You've found two actors who both fill your needs. Both are in their middle fifties, both have the heavy set, but kindly look of the country priest, and would elicit the desired response from the audience. Your third candidate is much younger, about thirty, Italian looking with a face that conveys an almost ascetic quality. You've picked his picture from the "unsuitable but interesting" file. Before you call your actors in, it is time to look at their resumes. Here they are:

JOHN MILLER
Tel 462-8157

Height: 5'8" Hair: Grey
Weight: 180 Eyes: Blue

FILM:

The Bold Ones	Universal
Freebie and the Bean	Warner Bros.
Battlestar Galactica	Universal
American Gigolo	Paramount
Sweepstakes	Paramount

TELEVISION:

Battlestar Galactica	Universal
Mork and Mindy	ABC-TV
Laverne and Shirley	ABC-TV
Best of the West	Paramount
Charlie's Angels	Spelling-Goldberg

COMMERCIALS: List upon request

**SPECIAL
ABILITIES:**   Tennis, swimming, golf

A very impressive list of credits—at first sight. But if you know how to "read" a resume, most of the things impressing you will vanish quickly into thin air. Let's go step by step through John Miller's resume.

John apparently has no agent representing him. He lists no agent's name in the left hand corner of his resume and gives out his own telephone number. This by itself is unimportant—there are many actors "in between" agents. Next you will notice that he is non-union. Fine, you are shooting a non-union film and are unable to hire union actors. However, since John is non-union, how could he appear in all those big feature films and known television shows? It is very obvious, only as a member of SAG (Screen Actors Guild) could he have worked on those productions. Well, did dear old John lie? No, he didn't. It is the gospel truth that he appeared on all of those films and television shows. But, he appeared as an *extra*—not an actor. Unfortunately, all the films he worked on as an extra should *not* be listed on his actor's resume. Extra work does count as experience, but it does not prove acting abilities. Yes, there are many excellent actors doing extra work because it pays their bills and keeps a roof over their heads, but they do not list this source of income on their resume. Listing his extra work on his actor's resume shows John off as a rank beginner.

76

John has experience in tennis, swimming and golf, and he has done some commercials. Again, since no additional information is given about his commercial credits, he must have been employed as an extra.

There is no information about any stage work he may have done. There is no mention about any workshops, courses, or classes he might have attended. The producer is informed about the following:

1. John did extensive work as an extra or atmosphere player.
2. He has not prepared himself for his chosen field by attending any acting classes.
3. He has no stage experience.

In conclusion, the producer knows that John is a working extra who wants to get a foothold as actor. Since John has no formal training it would be unwise to hire him. He would take up too much of the director's time and too much of the production time while groping to get his lines and actions right. The low-budget film simply cannot afford to be the proving ground for amateur actors.

The wise producer will not call him in for an interview, unless John's type is so perfect for the part that it pays to rewrite the script by giving John's lines to another character.

Our next candidate is Al Smith.

Rainbow Agency 654 Sunset Lane Hollywood, CA	**AL SMITH** **AFTRA**	Height: 5'7" Hair: Grey Weight: 178 Eyes: Hazel
FILM:	The Broken Arrow	Featured: UCLA Grad Thesis
STAGE:	Mutiny Court Marshall	Hickory Summer Theatre, Yosemite
	Oklahoma	Players Dinner Theatre, Encino
	Sabrina Fair	Los Angeles Theatre, LosAngeles
	Fiddler On The Roof	Players Dinner Theatre, Encino
	Night Of The Iguana	Hill Players, Oakland

TRAINING: The American Theatre Wing, NYC, NY
Los Angeles Valley College, Van Nuys
The Lee Strasberg Institute, Hollywood

SPECIAL ABILITIES: Race car driving, wrestling

Granted, Al's resume does not look nearly as impressive as John's but at least it inspires some confidence in the producer. First of all, Al has an agent representing him. Never mind that the agent is small and unknown, at least someone has the confidence that Al can do the job. Al has invested in joining a union, AFTRA (AMERICAN FEDERATION OF RADIO AND TELEVISION ARTISTS), and he has studied at well-known and respected schools. So far so good. Still, the producer will have some misgivings about Al's professional aptitude. Since he omits listing the parts he has played on stage, these might have been small and inconsequential. On the plus side is the fact that he worked for the Players Dinner Theatre twice. His film credits are weak. Only one student film is listed in which Al had a small part. Considering all of Al's credits, the producer knows the following:

1. Al has a fair professional background as stage actor.
2. He most likely will bring an interesting interpretation to the priest's role. After all he studied under good teachers.
3. He has practically no experience in film acting, and might have difficulties adjusting to the requirements of the camera.
4. Being a stage actor, his acting might look overblown and unbelievable on the screen.

Only if Al is the type the producer is looking for, will he call him in for an interview.

Lastly, let's take a look at Bill Sanders, whose picture emerged out of the "unsuitable but interesting" file.

BILL SANDERS
Tel 568-3487

Height: 5'7" Hair: Brown
Weight: 150 Eyes: Brown

FILM: Something from Nothing   Featured: USC
Thesis Film

The Apache Story   Co-starring: UCLA
Grad film

	Nickel and Dimes	Co-starring: Moorpark College
	Joe Comes Home	Co-starring: AFI, Los Angeles
INDUSTRIALS:	Telephone Repair	A&T Telephone Co., Los Angeles
	Management Manual	P&D Mfg. Co., Los Angeles
STAGE	Cinderella--King	Los Angeles Pierce College
	Odd Couple--Oscar	Los Angeles Valley College
	Detectives--Jarvis	Actor's Corner, Hollywood

TRAINING
Pierce College, Los Angeles, Film Acting
Valley College, Los Angeles, Advanced Acting
Lee Strasberg Institute (present)
Robert Falkner's Commercial Acting Workshop
(present)

Immediately, the producer knows he is dealing with a beginner. But this beginner has prepared himself, he is ready to be hired on a professional basis. Reading Bill Sander's resume, the producer is confident of the following facts:

1. Bill's fairly new on the scene, or he would have an agent representing him.
2. Bill has prepared himself in the best possible ways for his acting career:
      a. He has taken film as well as stage acting classes.
      b. He has studied under well-known teachers.
3. Since he played important parts in student films, Bill will survive in front of the camera.
4. Since he played fairly demanding parts on the college and equity waiver stage, Bill will be able to interpret his role in a professional way.

Most definitely, the producer will call in Bill for an interview, and it stands to reason that Bill will pass the interview and reading with flying colors.

Interview

Once you have decided on about four to five candidates for each role to be cast, you are ready to call in your actors to be interviewed. These interviews should never take place in the producer's or director's home. In case you do not work out of an office, you may do well to rent a conference room for this important occasion. Someone should be in attendance, to write down the actors' names and to hand out scenes to be read, while you and the director interview the actors.

In most cases, it is not necessary for the low-budget film producer to hire a casting director, unless he is truly unable to judge the actors' abilities. It is also unwise to invite the writer to the casting session. He is too close to the material and he may be argumentative. Listening to him, you might lose out on some exciting casting choices.

When interviewing your actors, you will observe:

1. Does he or she look like the picture submitted to you? At times, leading ladies will send a picture taken several years ago, and which is no longer representative of their looks.

2. Does the actor convey the same vitality he displayed in his picture? The main complaint of casting directors, directors and producers alike is that actors lack the "life" they show on their pictures.

3. Is the actor's personality genuine, or something he adopted for the interview?

4. Are there any signs of nervousness or insecurity? Does he clear his throat? Does she fiddle with her jewelry or hair? Is there any tension in hands or feet?

It is the actor's job to give you the confidence to hire him. He must be relaxed, alert, and exude a feeling of security. In short, he must enjoy the interview. Unfortunately, few actors do, and many will fall by the wayside during the preliminary interview. Of the five to ten candidates for each role, only three might be left.

The next step is the reading. For each part to be cast you'll have chosen an excerpt from a short scene. Now you will be in for your next surprise. Many of the actors who had given you confidence during the initial interview will read unsatisfactorily for the following reasons:

1. The reading turns out to be dull, revealing nothing of the actor's own vitality or personality.

2. The reading might be "acty" and artificial.

3. The reading will be "general." That is, it will have vitality and color, timing and rhythm, but suddenly, the likable person across from you becomes an "actor."

The best reading is easy. It has a natural flow which is unique to the actor's own personality, and still the actor remains aware of his responsibility to bring a character to life. Most importantly, the actor is more concerned about what the character *does* than what he *feels,* and he communicates the character's intention using his (the actor's) feelings as a launching pad. The most effective readings are conversations. If you audition a skilled actor, you will never be given the impression that he is reading words someone else wrote. You will always sense that the words the actor speaks are his own, expressing his own feelings and thoughts. He will make you believe that everything he says and does happens out of the spur of the moment, that he possesses the important quality of *immediacy.*

Most likely you will find the quality of immediacy in a only handful of actors. You cannot base your entire casting process on these gifted actors.

Callback

You will give the chance of a "callback" to these actors who are right in looks and type, and who gave a satisfactory reading. SAG ruling demands that for a callback the individual scripts must be made available a day ahead of the second interview. This is a wise ruling as it gives the talented actor the time and leisure to work on his scene. I always try to give my prospective actors about three days to study their scenes.

Hopefully, the actor has worked on the script, and the scene will have at least some trace of the quality you desire. In any event, now the director has the time to work with the actor. He will discuss the character and will give the actor some suggestions, subtly finding out whether the actor is able to take directions. You might have to call your main characters in for several readings before you'll be able to decide. You should read your minor characters twice.

If you are casting an union film you will have to pay rehearsal fees after the second interview. It is money well spent because it takes several interviews to get a sense of the actor's capabilities.

Once you have settled on about three choices for all leading parts and two choices for all minor characters, you are ready to video tape your actors. The frowned upon "screen test" of bygone days had its place, and so has the video taping of today. You never really know how an actor comes across on the screen. There is some intangible magic that transforms some actors into movie actors. Some women or men who are rather ordinary looking suddenly come alive in front of the camera—they have a certain presence, a sort of charisma that sets them apart from other actors. Others may be efficient but rather humdrum during rehearsals, yet once you see their performance on screen it will grip you. Vice versa, there are beautiful actors and actresses who seem to have that magic touch during rehearsals, yet come across as bland once you see them on screen. There is something more to the art of film acting than having a pretty face and an acceptable acting technique, and it is up to you as the producer and the director to discover this "something."

A video callback is also important, as it will reveal some of the more jarring mannerisms and facial difficulties actors are prone to:

Tension around mouth and eyes.

Keeping chin too far up or down.

Involuntary eye movement before speaking lines.

Keeping mouth open after lines have been spoken.

Head and shoulder movements that are too quick, giving the actor a nervous appearance.

Dull facial expression.

Over-active facial expression.

Nervous body movement in a medium shot.

Disregarding the confinements of the close-up.

Once the actor is aware of his mannerisms, it is the director's responsibility to straighten out these flaws. However, these faults have to be eliminated before principal photography begins. Ineffective camera performances should be corrected during rehearsal, not on the shoot.

Composition of Cast

Once you have found the best actors possible, you will have to match faces and personalities with the finesse of an artist. Ideally, each face and each personality contrasts with the rest of the cast. The actors should stand out individually, yet they should blend with the rest of the cast, as each actor compliments the others. If your film calls for three pretty girls to go on a vacation, they should not all be blondes. You will cast a blonde, a redhead and a brunette. Unless so desired for plot development, you will have them pretty much the same height and age. Child actors should be cast so that they look somewhat like their movie parents. If you are faced with the task of casting a group of characters such as a group of soldiers, college students, or businessmen, you'll have to cast actors who will form a homogeneous group but still retain their individuality. Go to a museum and take a look at old Dutch paintings and you will see what I mean.

In my film "Hell Riders,"* we had to cast a group of outlaw bikers. Granted bikers have a certain look. All the films that I viewed catered to that look, but James Bryan, the director, and I agreed that our bikers ought to be more individualized as they stood against a similar homogeneous group of townspeople. In the first draft of the script all our bikers seemed very much alike. The process of individualizing them did not start until we started casting. In the case of "Hell Riders," it was actually the actors who crystallized the various characters. Snake, their leader, displayed psychopathic behavior. His opponent, Convict—a tall but agile man—contrasted interestingly in looks, speech and movement with Stubby, his "yes" man and aide. The teenager, Rocky, was contrasted with the sly personality of Father, the defrocked minister. Once the group of "Hell Riders" was set, it was easy to adjust dialogue and physical actions to their individual characteristics.

*"Hell Riders" a Ciara Production, released by 21st Century Distribution Corporation, NYC.

Rehearsal

The director should have faith in his actors. He should encourage them in their own discoveries. He must be the one to lead each actor to a conclusion that is beneficial to the unity of the film. He should never allow his actors to go off on their own tangents, and one actor should not be permitted to overshadow the others. Rod Steiger points out, "A good director is like a good psychiatrist. He knows what conclusion he wants you to reach, but he lets you discover it for yourself."

Rehearsals, a luxury television seldom offers, are mandatory for the feature film. Each scene is shot so much out of sequence that the actors should be given the comfort of rehearsing the film in sequence, pretty much like a stage play.

The intensive rehearsal offers the actors the possibility to shade their work, to think about subtleties, to practice reactions. In short, to create three-dimensional characters. At times, it is one line, one look, or one movement that brings a scene into focus. The director is the one and only person who decides about the correct interpretation of each sequence. Yet, for all the talk about "correct interpretation" the good director knows there is not only one way to do things right. Any scene, any film can be done in a million ways. It's possible that many of them are "correct."

During rehearsals, the director will find out about the actors' techniques, about the way they are working, and what makes them tick. Some actors, coming from the Stanislavsky method, work in sense memory and affective memory. Others are more technically oriented. Some actors learn their lines, but refuse to do any more "homework." Once they are on the set they fuse themselves completely with their characters. Being fully aware of the different schools of acting, the director knows he will have to work differently with each actor. He also knows that he has to mold many different individuals into a unity that will blend effectively with the mood and theme—specifically, the unity of the film.

Stars

If you do a small, very low-budget film you do not need any name actors. The fact is you could not afford them. But once your films get bigger, once the budget is much higher, you will consider having some "name" heading your cast.

Should you consider casting a name, then your company must be signatory with SAG—you must pay SAG scale to all actors. You must comply with SAG rules for all actors. Adding a name to your cast list will bring up the cost of your film considerably. At this point, you must decide whether or not it is worth it to add a name. There are two schools of thought concerning this issue. One states that in today's film market the name, unless it is a big one, doesn't matter at all. "The story counts" is claimed over and over. The other side states that no distributor will look at a film unless it is headed by a "star."

Both sides are right, and both sides are wrong. The truth lies somewhat in the middle. Yes, distributors still ask, "Who is in it?" meaning,

83

"Do you have a star?" And it is easier to sell a good picture if you have a name actor in it. But even if you have an "all star—no name cast," will you make a sale if your picture is poor, and your story line boring? The time of the "star picture" has passed. There are few actors left who draw audiences on the strength of their name only. Clint Eastwood is one, Charles Bronson another. The days of the Clark Gable, Marilyn Monroe and Doris Day picture are gone. Audiences now flock to the theatres because a picture is "different," as the success of "Star Wars," "ET" and "Jaws" proved, films which feature mind-boggling special effects, movement and action. Of course, films like "Raiders of the Lost Ark" are an impossible dream for the low-budget producer. He has to deal with dollars and cents, not mega-bucks. It is interesting to observe that all the motion pictures mentioned above did not have what one may term "stars," but made stars of good but pedestrian actors.

Contracting a star might be a time consuming, but rather easy task. It is your responsibility, not the director's, to hire the name. First you'll look through your "bible," the *Academy Players Directory*. The Directory lists most well-known and not so well-known actors and actresses, shows their pictures, and gives the names of their agents and personal managers. By the way, the Directory should be on every producer's desk. It is your status symbol. It shows the world that you are a "working" producer.

You will zoom in on several stars whom you consider right for the lead. You will not contact the stars, but speak with their agents. Some stars will not be available because of other commitments. Some may feel that your company is too unknown, while others ask for too much money. After only a few telephone calls (yes, once I replaced a leading lady with another name actress within three hours), you will have several agents interested.

Your next step is to send the script to the agent, who will turn it over to his client. It is now up to the star to accept or decline. As soon as the star has accepted the script, you'll send a check which will be held in trust by the agent. The check will be accompanied by a contract. It is better if you write the contract—don't leave this task to the star's agent, or you may be sorry later on.

It is best to go for a "Play and Pay" contract, meaning that the actor will not receive his salary unless he works the designated number of days. Some agents do everything in their power to have you sign an agreement guaranteeing their stars' salaries (and their commissions) in case you have to postpone or cancel your film. Stay away from these contracts. It is easier to find a new star than to be obligated to pay for services not received.

Shortly after the agent and the star have accepted your script, have had time to look over the contract, and have made certain your company is solvent, you will meet with the star. This meeting will take place in the agent's office. Now is the time for the star to bring in his requests, the changes in costume, the changes in lines, the request for special make-up, and so on. These requests are more or less symbolic in nature. The star probes the borderline of his power. He finds out how far you will bend.

You in turn take a good look at the star, determine whether the leading lady is as pretty as her picture and her other films suggest, and whether the leading man is as rugged looking as you had hoped. Once everything is settled to everyone's satisfaction, the actual work begins. The contract is signed by both sides. Rehearsal times, make-up testing, and fittings are arranged.

Most of the stars I have worked with are a delight and a pleasure to know. They are professionals, come on time, and do not complain about some of the discomforts associated with low-budget film production. They give their all during long and hard shooting hours. Yes, they are pros, true troopers and enthusiastic motion picture actors.

Chapter Seven
About Acting

Actors are the most important part of the complicated matrix called a motion picture. They know it, and at times try to throw their weight around. The director, the producer, and even the distributor have to depend on them, because actors are the ones who make the writer's story physically perceptible. An enormous amount of money rides on their talent, responsibility and dependability. They all have the personal obligation to themselves and to the production company to give their best. It is their duty to do their homework, to present mankind and human emotion on a heightened level. The actor should not be as interested in himself as he is in the part. That makes a big difference. That is his job. That is what he is supposed to do.

I have had the opportunity of working with many actors and can attest to the difficulties cropping up between a director and even the most knowledgeable and skilled actors. Arguments erupt during rehearsal, and worse, during the shoot. The director wants a certain result, but fails to see that the actor is unable to read the road signs leading to the result. Difficulties are likely to occur because of some hidden reasons in the actor's psychological makeup. At this point, I am only discussing obstacles faced by the skilled professional actor; I am referring neither to the beginner nor to the amateur.

Most actors approach their roles from two different points of departure. They either search for the character's "feeling" at any given point, or they immerse themselves completely in the role, contending happily, "I lived through all of this myself. The character on the written page is ME." (Let's clarify that I am not referring to the *presentational* or *representational* styles of acting which belong on the stage, but to the naturalistic approach employed by the trained motion picture actor.) Both points of departure will result in unrewarding screen performances.

The actor who structures the interpretation of his role upon the character's "feeling" is like the builder who builds a house without proper foundation. Emotions like happiness, anger, sadness, contentment are a reaction to some motivating force. Without such a motivating force, no emotion or feeling can exist. For this very reason, feelings cannot be produced at will. They are the human reaction to some goal that has been frustrated or satisfied. This goal might be miniscule or gargantuan in its dimension. It might be Hannibal trying to catch a fly, or Hannibal struggling to cross the Alps. You see, the goal itself is immaterial. What counts is our reaction to it.

Picture, if you will, a beautiful summer day. The sunshine beckons you to leave your home and go to the beach. You have done all your work (goal-satisfied) and you will reward yourself with a day off. You are in a happy mood. Just as you leave the room the telephone rings summoning you to a conference, you will spend the afternoon in a stuffy office instead on the sunny beach (goal-frustrated), and naturally your mood turns sour.

Actors who work off the feeling of their characters often disregard the reasons which caused these feelings. They also forget that feelings cannot be produced at will, but depend on the satisfaction-frustration process. Summoning emotions on command will result in the "acty," overblown, and therefore unbelievable performance in front of the camera. Unfortunately, the actors are—at least most of the time—painfully aware of their fake emotions. They try to reach true emotion by "pushing" the artificial emotion they are expressing. In turn, their performance becomes increasingly artificial.

The actor who approaches his role by completely identifying with the character does not fare much better. Even though the character's emotional makeup may be similar to the actor's, even though circumstances and events are close to the ones having touched the actor's life, the fact remains that the actor's job is to *portray a fictional character*, not himself.

The concept of "taking over the character and making him myself" has many followers among film actors. This kind of thinking has generated many myths among actors. Some actors see their goal in what one may call "minimum behavior"—they are so relaxed in front of the camera that their performances become colorless. They never really *commit* themselves to the expression of any one thought or feeling. There is no challenge to their work. Other actors, proscribing to the same concept, work extremely hard. They go to great lengths to fuse themselves with the character. In this process, their acting becomes *internalized;* the actor acts for himself not for the audience. The actor will give a performance that is emotionally demanding of himself, but not gripping to the audience.

It is unfortunate that in all the above instances the actor is concerned in a very self-centered way about his own emotions and forgets about the audience. A great performance involves three entities:

The character as *written* by the playwright
PLUS:
The character as *envisioned* by the actor
RESULTS IN:
The character as *experienced* by the audience

Looking at the actor's performance in this respect we see it cannot exist without the audience's participation. It is the director's obligation to lead the actor to a way of expressing himself that is simple, clear to the audience, and expresses the writer's purpose. During the course of the first rehearsals, all main characters involved in a film should be encouraged to approach their individual work within the same frame of reference. The script should be researched on the following levels:

87

Facts and logical assumptions.
Goal and sub-goals.
Personalization.
Positive and negative response.
Train of thought.
Images and sense memories.

It is interesting to observe that feeling and emotion, the two seemingly agitating forces in the art of acting, are not mentioned in the list. It was Stanislavsky's great discovery that emotions *should not* be part of the actor's search for the role to be performed. His conclusion was that emotion has to emerge spontaneously.

Emotion will flow forth spontaneously if it stems from the motive and reaction process inherent in all good acting. Yet, to reach this point one has to go through the steps outlined above.

Facts and Logical Assumptions

After reading the script through quickly, you will have to step away from it, and from the character you are about to portray. Close your mind to all the prejudice you may have about the character. You neither like nor dislike the role you have been cast for. I know this is difficult to do, but try anyway. Your first acting obligation is to get to know the character as an entity. Stay away from injecting anything of yourself into it at this moment. Do some detective work, find out everything you possibly can about this woman or man who soon will be you. You will achieve this by looking for the facts inherent in the script. The facts are:

What a character says about himself.
What other characters say about the character to be portrayed.

Let's assume you have been cast to play LIL STANHOPE in my film "FROZEN SCREAM." The next three pages are the first scene in which she appears, as she meets her adversary DETECTIVE McGUIRE. You will now make a list of all the facts apparent in this scene.

INTERCOM
(V.O.)
Dr. Stanhope to the nurses station . . .
Dr. Stanhope.

Lil looks up and walks faster. She approaches the station and speaks to the Nurse at the desk. A man also stands at the desk.

LIL
Yes, Meg?

                              MEG
              Doctor, I'm sorry to bother you, but
              this man . . .

ANGLE on McGuire.

                              MEG
                       (continuing O.S.)
              . . .has been impatient about talking
              to you.

Lil is now looking at McGuire.

                              LIL
              Can I help you?

McGuire pulls out his I.D.

                            McGUIRE
              Dr. Stanhope, I'm Detective McGuire.
              I'm here on a routine investigation.
              I was wondering if you might answer a
              few questions?

Meg turns back to her work.

                              LIL
              What sort of investigation?

                            McGUIRE
              Well now, it seems some former students
              of yours have been missing . . . a Bob
              Russell and a Richard Kirk. Their landlady
              thought they were skipping rent . . .

He hands her their photographs. Lil takes them and looks.

                            McGUIRE
                          (continuing)
              . . . but, some checking has gone on, and it
              seems, no one has seen them since your
              last seminar at the university.

As Lil looks at the photos, there is a slight expression of recognition that
quickly gives way to a transparent smile.

LIL

I have so many young people in my class,
but I think I do remember these boys. Very
bright they were. I was wondering why
they hadn't signed up for my new course.

Lil hands the pictures back to McGuire.

McGUIRE

Yes, well we were wondering that also. A few
of their friends said they were very fond of
you and Dr. Jonson. They went out with you
once or twice, didn't they?

LIL

Not in a social sense, some of my classes
incorporate trips to special locations.

McGUIRE

I see, neither of the boys had any family to
speak of but, uh, Russell was having a
relationship with a young Med student, Lisa
Cocran . . . do you know her?

Lil is becoming concerned.

McGUIRE

Well, I guess they were sort of boyfriend,
girlfriend and she said that Bob was
participating in some sort of drug
consciousness program headed by you
and Dr. Jonson.

LIL
(stern)
That class was on expanded consciousness.

McGUIRE

Is there a difference?

LIL

Our experiments were on the order of mental
concepts and exercises. Completely free of
drugs, including cigarettes and alcohol.

McGUIRE

If you say so, I'm sure it's true, but this Lisa
did mention drugs.

LIL
If these boys were using drugs it wasn't with
my knowledge or approval...

Facts

1. Lil is being paged.
2. Lil is a physician.

3. Lil works in a hospital.
4. Lil is being asked some questions by the police.
5. Lil has students.

6. Two of her students are missing.

7. Lil is teaching at a university.
8. The students attended Lil's seminar.

9. Lil recognizes the students.

10. Lil states she has many students, she smiles.
11. McGuire states that the students were fond of Lil.
12. Lil is associated with a Dr. Jonson.
13. Her classes incorporate trips to special locations.

14. Both boys had no family, but one had a girlfriend.
15. Lil teaches a class on expanded consciousness.
16. The girlfriend mentioned that drugs were used.

17. Lil denies the drug use.

Logical Assumptions

1. No Assumption.
2. She is a professional with extensive training.
3. She is experienced in her field.
4. She might be involved in something or she may know something.
5. She must be very knowledgeable in her profession.
6. She must be involved in something, she is *too* concerned.
7. None.
8. She knows them, so why is she not worried.
9. She should have recognized their names.
10. She is evasive. There is no reason for smiling.
11. Again, why did she not recognize them right away?
12. She must be someone important.
13. She associates with her students. Why did it take so long for her to recognize the boys?
14. No one would pay much attention if they were to disappear.
15. She must be a psychologist.

16. Possibly the girlfriend lied. But if she didn't lie, something sinister is going on.
17. None.

Once all facts have been discovered, the actor will put his own interpretations, his own logical assumptions next to the facts. Dissecting an entire script, scene for scene, will give him a composite picture of the character. From this one scene alone we will get the following composite about Lil Stanhope:

She is a psychologist.
She teaches classes at a university and is on the staff of a hospital.
She is well-educated, fairly affluent, and probably has reached her
   middle thirties.
She is involved in some kind of research that the police are
   questioning her about.

No husband is mentioned, therefore she may dedicate her life to her
work.

From these observations, the actress portraying Lil Stanhope will
draw these conclusions:

Lil is on her own turf in the hospital, her movements are self-assured.
Her voice tells us she is used to commanding respect.
Her eyes tell us that she is accustomed to looking at people and
things closely before she makes any decision.
She might be involved in something beyond her control, but her
profession has probably taught her to stand up well under pressure.

These first conclusions will give the actress a handle on Lil's character. Yet, without the established correlation between facts and logical assumptions, the actress might have been tempted to give the plot away by
playing the *result of being scared.* Yes, in all probability Lil is scared. It
is obvious that she might be involved in something sinister, but our investigation showed us that she is holding up, she never *reveals* any fear.

Main Goal and Sub-goals

As soon as you have "met" the character, it is time to find out about
what he is going to do—what his goal, intention, or main action is. These
three terms, *goal, intention* and *main action* point to the road he is
going to take, which in the course of interpretation leads to the decisions
he has to make. Each script, stageplay and book deals with the goals of
the respective characters and with the satisfaction or frustration of these
intentions. Let's look at some of the goals we encounter in literature:

Blanche DuBois—"A Streetcar Named Desire"
I want to rest from the tribulations and disappointments I
experienced.
Scarlett O'Hara—"Gone with the Wind"
I want to fight to get the man I love and to keep my plantation.
Oliver Twist—"Oliver Twist"
I want to survive, regardless of what I'll have to do.
Amanda—"The Glass Menagerie"
I want to close my eyes to reality.

You'll have noticed that each goal listed starts with: "I want" and
adds an *action* verb. The character must decide to do something, he
must decide on an action to keep the ball rolling. Each main goal must
have the appropriate sub-goal. This sub-goal should be established in
each scene. Again, the sub-goal may be the impetus to a series of sub-
goals. Sub-goals should strengthen the main goal, and both main goal as

well as sub-goal must be strong enough to agitate interesting actions (i.e. acting).

It is fairly easy to establish a main goal for Lil Stanhope. Take a look at the scene where she meets Detective McGuire. We know she is involved in some shady experiments and should be blamed for the students' disappearances. Naturally she wants remain free of blame. Her main goal in this scene might be one of the following:

I want to explain.
I want to hide.
I want to take control.

I want to explain would constitute a weak and uninteresting goal. One may explain a missed plane or an unbalanced checkbook, but for this particular scene the main goal, *I want to explain* would cause an uninteresting interpretation of the scene.

I want to hide is somewhat better. Still, this main goal is misleading in the sense that it would reveal Lil's fear too early. The audience might guess, but they should not know.

I want to control is the best choice so far, as it encapsulizes Lil's personality. Remember, we meet her for the first time in this scene, and it is important that the audience gets a clear picture of who the lady is. Even more importantly, *I want to control* gives the actress portraying Lil Stanhope the choice of many interesting subgoals:

I want to impress.
I want to brush off.
I want to disregard.
I want to set straight.
I want to remove myself.

Personalization

So far so good. Yet, it is more than likely that the actress, Joan, playing the role of Lil Stanhope faces an impasse. She never has been involved in any sinister research. The strongest drug she ever took was an aspirin, and the fact is, she has no personal point of departure to believably portray the good psychologist believably. This is where the technique of personalization is helpful. The actor simply finds an equation between:

What the *character* wants
                and
What the *actor* feels

The fusion of these factors gives rise to an entirely new being:
The character as portrayed

Lil Stanhope is in control of herself, a fact which is not difficult for Joan to portray. This is the way she conducts herself most of the time. In this respect, she *is* Lil Stanhope. But underneath Lil's calm exterior burns a nagging fear.

Joan has to portray this fear. She, as a person, has never experienced anything similar to what Lil goes through. She has no frame of reference. It's possible that her interpretation of the fear Lil experiences will be shallow at best. Should Joan decide simply to portray "fear" then her performance will become overblown and acty, since Joan plays an emotion without having a reason or motive for such feeling. Personalization should be used at this point of preparation. It is true, Joan cannot portray honestly the emotion felt during a situation alien to her. She has never experienced anything even closely related to this scene. Yet, each and every one of us, including Joan, will remember instances when we were afraid, but had to control ourselves. Maybe Joan will remember the day in Traffic Court when she fought against an unjust ticket, and the police officer accused her of coloring the truth. Yes, she was trembling, but kept her cool. If Mary were to play the part of Lil, she might recall the day when her boss accused her of having misplaced a file.

The fact of the matter is that the incident the actor lived through might only be remotely related to the incident he has to portray. Once the actor has arrived at a correlation between *real incident* and *scene*, he will try to remember what he experienced. He will ask himself:

Did I feel any physical discomfort during the real incident?
Did I feel any emotional discomfort?
How did the clothes on my body feel?

Joan might have felt a heaviness in her chest. Maybe she had difficulties swallowing and her voice was strained, while Mary fought hard to control her trembling hands, and suddenly felt that the scarf around her neck was choking her.

Recalling that the actor portrays the character's goal and the actor's emotion, it should not be difficult for Joan and Mary to endow Lil with the emotions they experienced.

Positive and Negative Reaction

It is a psychological fact that we have only *two reactions* to any given circumstance. We either like something—we are *positive* about it, or we dislike something—we are *negative* about it. This positive-negative spectrum embraces all emotions that a human being experiences. A positive reaction might be as negligible as the sense of comfort you experience while drinking a cup of coffee or tea, or it might be as all engulfing as the ecstatic joy and happiness that fills your soul when you find the person you really love, hold your child in your arms, receive the college degree you worked so hard for, sign for the coveted role in a film, and so on.

The negative reaction works the same way—moving from the minuscule experience of being stuck in traffic, to the magnitude of despair of seeing your life's dream shattered.

Your body adjusts to the positive or negative reaction. During a positive situation your body is relaxed, you may smile. During a negative reaction your body grows tense. Just remember the other day on the beach. Wasn't your body relaxed as you happily watched the surf? But how about yesterday at the dentist's office? How did your body feel as Dr. Miller reached for the drill and said, "Now open wide"? I bet your body grew rigid.

Taking for granted the mental positive or negative reaction and the accompanying physical relaxation or tension, we will move one step ahead. Many actors give an unbelievable performance because they act only with their faces—they remain blissfully unaware that in life, their entire bodies react, and their entire bodies should react when acting. It is the actor's obligation to decide how he (not the character) would physically react during any given situation. The actor's oral statement will automatically match his physiological statement. If his body is relaxed, his voice will sound happy and friendly, then angry or cold, or possibly afraid, the moment his body grows tense.

Let's take another look at the Lil Stanhope scene. We already have established her main goal—to keep control—and her sub-goals—to impress, to brush off, to disregard. It is easy to decide that the entire scene is negative. Joan's body will be tense, resulting in her voice sounding angry or cold. Wait a moment—didn't we decide on *"to keep control"* as her main goal? True, most of the scene is negative, but there must be sufficient moments of relaxation (control) or dear Detective McGuire knows right away where the rat is buried. Wouldn't it be more believable if moments of tension were to be contrasted by moments of consciously forced relaxation?

The beginning of the scene might look something like this:

INTERCOM
(V.O.)
Dr. Stanhope to the nurse's station . . .
. . . Dr. Stanhope . . .

Lil looks up and walks faster (her body is relaxed, there is a smile on her face). She approaches the station and speaks to the nurse. A man also stands at the desk.

LIL

Yes, Meg?

MEG
Doctor, I am sorry to bother you, but
this man . . .

ANGLE on McGUIRE

MEG
(V.O.)
. . . has been impatient to talk to you.

Lil is now looking at McGuire (her body is still relaxed, but she doesn't
smile any longer).

LIL
Can I help you?

McGUIRE pulls out his ID (Lil's body grows tense in anticipation).

McGUIRE
Dr. Stanhope, I'm Detective McGuire.

At this point, Lil's body grows even tenser. There is a slight indication of
physical discomfort. She might swallow, look away, or adjust the scarf
around her neck.

McGUIRE
I am here on a routine investigation.
I was wondering if you might answer
a few questions?

Lil has won control over herself. She forces her body to relax, but she
doesn't smile.

LIL
What sort of investigation?

Train of Thought

In life we always think. We consider facts, we weigh pros and cons, we
try to remember—the list of thoughts going through our brains is
endless. At times we are not even aware of this continuous process. Just
ask anyone, "What did you eat for lunch?" and you may not receive an
immediate answer. The person you've asked will look at you, then turn
away, and look back at you again before giving you the earth shaking
reply, "Nothing, I'm on a diet." The point is, even to give an answer
about something as mundane as lunch, he had to think.

We do not know precisely the next word, or even the next sentence,
we will say. The actor, however, does. He has learned his lines. He not

96

only knows his speech, but his partner's speech as well. For the actor there is no need to think. Omitting thoughts often robs the actor of immediacy. Only if you add thought patterns to your lines will the audience get the feeling that everything on the screen is happening right now.

Thought patterns may be positive or negative in nature, the same as the spoken word.

Thought patterns might be placed before, in the middle, or after a line.

Thought patterns must be supported by genuine thoughts—they are not "holes" through which an actor stares into space.

Again, let's go back to the Lil Stanhope scene. This time we will take a look at Detective McGuire's first speech, adding his thoughts.

THOUGHT: *Hey, a good looking lady this Doctor Stanhope.*
SPOKEN: Dr. Stanhope, I'm Detective McGuire.

THOUGHT: *Kind of embarrassing to question her.*
SPOKEN: I'm here on a routine investigation.

THOUGHT: *Come on McGuire get hold of yourself, do your duty.*
SPOKEN: I was wondering if you might answer a few questions?

Thoughts run much faster than words. They should enhance your lines, but never drag. Thought patterns will give your partner the chance to listen and to react. They are the basis for motive and reaction, and in this sense the basis for effective and believable acting.

Images and Sense Memories

Method acting as conceived by Stanislavsky and defined by Lee Strasberg employs sense memory and image as its basic tools. A director has to be careful in introducing these concepts during rehearsal, unless the majority of his actors are well trained in this field. Sense memory and image differ as follows:

Sense memory is the *recalling* of *actual* things experienced through our senses:
Touch—petting a kitten
Smell—smelling a rose
Sight—seeing fireworks
Sound—listening to a band concert

Image is an *imagined* entity, only possible in the realm of our imagination:

Boiling lava in your stomach (anger)
Warm rays emerging out of your fingertips (compassion)
Daggers coming out of your eyes (hate)
Champagne bubbles floating through your body (joy)

It is easy to understand why a director should tackle even these very basic tools of expression only if an actor is thoroughly familiar with the techniques of method acting. Yet, if an actor is method-trained he should make every effort to incorporate his training. Both sense memory and images will result in a heightened, completely personalized, but simple and natural performance. The actor's expression will flow unforced, and truly from within. The reason for this is that the actor will not concentrate on his expression, but on the internal task (sense memory or image) resulting in that expression. As in life, the expression is the reaction to a motive.

To illustrate my point, let's take another (I promise, the last) look at the Lil Stanhope scene. We agreed upon her main goal, the subsequent sub-goals, and established that her physical reaction (most of the time) is negative. We know that the actress, Joan, will do an excellent job portraying Lil. But if Joan were to use some method acting tools, how much more exciting might the same scene be?

To express the sub-goal of I WANT TO IMPRESS, she might use the image of a steel rod running through her spine.

To express the sub-goal of I WANT TO DISREGARD, she might use the sense memory of touch, as she feels herself touching an ice cube.

Reasons Why Capable Actors Face Difficulties in Front of the Camera

Sometimes directors are puzzled about why capable actors who did well during rehearsals and the first shooting days, suddenly fall apart in front of the camera. While an actor's surprising incompetence may seem like a disaster, it really does not present an insurmountable obstacle, once the director gets to the root of the actor's difficulties:

Split concentration.
Dependence upon "inspiration."
Actor's own emotional state momentarily opposite to character's emotional state.
Fear of the camera.

Split Concentration
Split concentration occurs if the actor's concentration is not focused as much on his role as on the *effect* his work has on others. He might be so bent on impressing ("This performance will land me a lead in the next film."), he might be nervous ("If I blow my lines once more, they

will replace me."), and suddenly the actor's personal concerns will take over the character's goals.

Split concentration is the motion picture actor's worst enemy. The camera sees and registers everything. If the actor lacks full concentration, the audience will notice it.

Lee Strasberg told his students over and over, "Never be concerned about the HOW of your performance, simply concentrate on the WHAT." In other words, forget whether or not the director likes your work, but simply think about WHAT you are doing—concentrate on the momentary goal, the sense memory you may be working with, your body's positive or negative reaction to the given motive, your thought pattern.

I often think that stunt people are such great performers because they have to concentrate so completely upon their given tasks. The actor should approach his performance from the same point of full concentration. The fully concentrated state will prevent any nervousness. The moment the director senses a split concentration, it is his responsibility to lead the actor back to the WHAT.

Dependence upon Inspiration

At times, talented and creative actors fall into the "inspiration trap." They have done some homework regarding background investigation of the character, they know their lines, but otherwise leave everything up to the moment. They take their responses from whatever forces them to respond at this moment. It may be the heat in the studio, it may be the happiness they feel about working, it may be the mean glint in the director's eyes.

Sometimes their way of approaching a role works magnificently, especially if they are working opposite another exciting actor their performance will be gripping. At other times, it will be general and bland, or worse—inconsistent with the requirements of the scene. Having an "inspirational" actor in the cast, one never really knows what to expect. The director who had familiarized himself with this particular actor's way of working should always be ready with a detailed outline of the actor's scene. The actor, in turn, must be willing to follow the director's specific instructions.

Actor's Emotional State Momentarily Opposite to Character's Emotional State

Besides being actors, we are human beings subject to our very own joy and sadness. You may have to play a tragic scene, but you yourself are ready to burst your seams out of happiness. Naturally, you are an actor or actress, you can "act" the sadness. Never mind. At times our own emotions are so much stronger than the ones we are supposed to portray that the combination of the two leads either to monotonous or pushed display of unbelievable emotion.

The good director will easily correct this fallacy by making the actor aware of the discrepancy, and by insisting on a definite positive or negative reaction.

Camera Fear

The director and the producer should find out during the video taped callback which of the candidates display fear of the camera. If an actor's reading was alive and communicative during the earlier readings, but becomes stiff once the camera is rolling, the director has to deal with camera fear. All beginning actors and some stage actors are bothered by this fear. Should the director decide to hire a camera shy actor anyway, he should break this fear before principal photography starts.

The camera shy actor is unable to communicate as he faces the camera. In this way, he builds a wall between the audience and himself. The director should explain to the actor that the camera is not in lieu of the audience, *it is not the audience, but it is the actor's partner*. In this respect, the camera is a person, the one with whom the actor is in love or angry.

It is not easy for anyone to view a mechanical device—such as a camera as a person. Nevertheless, all effective motion picture acting is based on this concept. A number of stars had perfected this communication to a point that it made them stars. Neither Marilyn Monroe nor Clark Gable were great artists, nor outstandingly good looking people for that matter, but they made love to the camera—they communicated their emotions in such a way that audiences all over the world were compelled to fall in love with them.

The camera shy actor must be taught to communicate with inanimate objects. First he must be able to talk to his pet (not difficult, we all talk to our cat or dog), then he should talk to a stuffed animal (a little harder, but still not impossible, who can resist a Garfield Cat?), then he should talk to a chair or lamp, and finally when he has proved to himself that he can communicate with his bedpost, he will be able to communicate with the camera.

CIARA PRODUCTIONS, INC.
U.S.A.

AGREEMENT

This agreement made on the _____ day of _____ 1983

between CIARA PRODUCTIONS, INC and _____ hereafter referred to as "Artist".

In consideration of the covenants and conditions herein contained, the parties agree as follows:

_____will render his/her services as _____

_____billing will be as _____
in the motion picture presently entitled HELL RIDERS. Artist hereby accepts his/her participation on the terms provided. Artists services shall be rendered on such locations as may be designated by CIARA PRODUCTIONS, INC.

Artists will receive the sum of _____

_____

Artist agrees not to request any additional payments of money. Artist agrees not to request neither percentage nor interest in any future distribution or sale of this film, be they foreign, domestic, television, cable or any other form of public or private viewing.

Artist stipulates that he/she has read this document, understood its meaning in full, and his/her signature warrants the understanding and acceptance of contract.

RENEE HARMON
President
CIARA PRODUCTIONS, INC.

101

Chapter Eight
The Producer's "Paper War"

The pre-production work on any picture involves budgetary considerations. Pre-production planning might require as little as three to four
weeks preparation, or it might require several months. In both cases the
eventual success or failure of a picture depends upon the quality of the
pre-production planning. The major studios, and even the big independent motion picture companies support large staffs working on budget
and pre-production, while you, the small, low-budget filmmaker, have to
depend on yourself to do all the work. Naturally, reports, lists and schedules have to be on a more modest scale. Nevertheless, do not omit any
of the suggested lists. All your pre-production planning has to be completed once you start shooting. Now is the time is to "get your house in
order."

The producer's "paper war" begins with the *script breakdown*. The
director has read the script and dissected each scene into so many
camera set-ups, indicated by numbers on the right and left hand side of
the script. These set-ups are only preliminary, and might be changed
during shooting. Still, they give you a clue to the number of days
required to complete principal photography. Next, the production
manager (in the case of the low-budget, small film you, the producer) will
underline all pertinent information to be transferred to the various
breakdowns and reports. It's likely that the following schedules will suffice
for your needs:

Continuity Breakdown
Breakdown Board
Shooting Schedule
Call Sheet
Location Breakdown
Crew List
Location List
Actor's List
Production Report (once principal photography has started)

Continuity Breakdown

The continuity breakdown contains *all* information necessary for
each sequence to be filmed. Each sequence should be listed on a separate sheet of paper. It should contain the following information:

Cast, bits and extras
Wardrobe for each cast member
Day or night shooting
Location
Special equipment and construction
Special effects
Sound effects
Props
Car, livestock, etc.
Total script pages
Scene number and synopsis

Upon completion of all the continuity breakdown sheets, the sheets are assembled in such a manner as to retain as much continuity as possible and still hold the shooting time to a minimum. By way of example, five scenes are scheduled for one location. Two scenes take place in the living room, one scene takes place on the patio, while the rest of the scenes will be filmed in the kitchen. The breakdown sheets will be arranged so that the first scenes to be filmed are the ones scheduled for the living room, then the camera crew will move on to the patio to continue shooting, while the lighting crew sets up the kitchen.

Breakdown Board

The information given on the breakdown sheets are transferred to the breakdown board—a large headboard listing all the various requirements. The locations are listed on individual colored strips along with cast, sequence, number of pages, vehicles, props and scene numbers. The strips are arranged in the same manner as the breakdown sheets.

It is true, the breakdown board adds immensely to the "look" of any production office, and is a requirement for the producer of the average budget production. On a bigger film the producer rarely visits the battle lines. He sits in his office and knows about the state of affairs by the way his production manager juggles the many colored stripes on his breakdown board. For the producer of the low-budget film such a board is unnecessary. He is out in the trenches anyway and knows what goes on. It is much more convenient for him to carry the breakdown sheets along with the script.

Shooting Schedule

Once the breakdown has been completed, and once the producer has arrived at the conclusion that his film should be completed after a given number of days, he would do well to call the director, stunt coordinator, the cinematographer, and the lighting director in for a meeting. They all should agree that the shooting schedule is reasonable and so many camera set-ups will be accomplished each day. It is important that everyone agrees on the shooting schedule. The final budget will reflect this schedule. Remember, each and every added day will burden the (usually extremely weak) budget unnecessarily.

After the number of shooting days have been agreed upon, the producer will inform the carpenter, the wardrobe mistress, and the prop department about his various requirements.

Call Sheet

The call sheet represents the total work done on any given day. In a bigger production, the call sheet is prepared by the assistant director, then approved by the director and finally given to the production manager who is responsible for the final approval. In the low-budget production, the call sheet, as so many other things, falls on your shoulders. Make out your call sheets ahead of time, simply penciling in the call times as needed.

A call sheet is issued each day to cast and crew for the following day's work. It includes the time and place where actors and crew have to report.

Location Breakdown

I find a location breakdown extremely helpful. This list includes the addresses of all locations utilized, as well as the addresses and telephone numbers of the following service units:

Film processing lab
Sound lab
Supplier of raw-stock
Caterer
Location permit office
Paramedics
Equipment rental house
Portable dressing rooms and/or toilets

Production Report

Once you are in production your daily production report will verify what has been completed (or, how far behind you are with your schedule). This report is important in terms of the over-all budget. It gives information about:

Number of scenes completed
Number of script pages completed
Amount of film consumed
Number of prints made
Number of minutes (actual screen time) shot
Number of camera set-ups
Total time the cast and the crew has worked

It is the production manager's responsibility to gather all the facts. In case you as producer serve as production manager as well, you should assign the production report to your script supervisor. The following pages will give examples of the discussed breakdowns and schedules, based on my screenplays* "Frozen Scream," directed by Frank Roach, and "Hell Riders," directed by James Bryan.

1. EXT—ROAD—NIGHT

A dense fog sways over the open road. Off to the side there are skeletal forms of partially obscured trees. All is grey and still. A faint illumination peers thru the mist and readily approaches the CAMERA until the lights of the car are revealed. The lights move forward until they fill the screen.

SUPER TITLE: THE CHILL FACTOR

2. INT—CAR—NIGHT

Cautiously maneuvering thru the fog is ANN GERRAD. She is in her mid-thirties, sensibly dressed and attractive. She strains her vision as if noticing something up ahead.

3. EXT—GAS STATION—NIGHT

Ann's car pulls into the gas station and parks. The ever present fog serves only to heighten the sense of desolation.

Ann gets out of the car and warily approaches the telephone booth. She enters and closes the door behind her.

4. INT—TELEPHONE BOOTH—NIGHT

Ann searches through her purse. She finds a coin, inserts it and dials. The phone buzzes and clicks as it is answered.

> ANN
> Tom darling, it's me again . . . yes, I'll be
> home in a while. The fog is very thick out
> here and it's kind of slowed me down.

*Both released by 21st Century Distribution Corporation, New York.

5. INT—GERRARD RESIDENCE/STUDY—NIGHT

ANGLE ON TOM GERRARD as he stands over his desk holding the
telephone with one hand and rummaging through the desk drawer with
the other. The dim light of the yellow desklight casts eerie shadows
around the room and over his worried face. In the distance we HEAR the
SOUND of HUMMING VOICES.

> TOM
>
> Ann, I worry about you when you drive up
> to see your folks. That's not the best of roads,
> even in good weather.

6. INT—PHONE BOOTH—NIGHT

> ANN
>
> Hey, I'm a big girl now, I can take care of
> myself, besides, I'm the one who's worried.
> When I called you earlier, you sounded so
> troubled, tense even.... Are you okay? I mean
> really okay?

Shooting Schedule

The shooting schedule reflects the final shooting script. Camera set-
ups are listed, and a time limit is given for each set-up. It is the production manager's responsibility to keep the show moving, specifically, to
keep the film on schedule. The low-budget production often omits the
position of the production manager, and it is the producer who has to
"tenderly" remind everyone that the schedule must be adhered to. The
following shooting schedule is taken from my film "Hell Riders." It was
an exterior shoot at Colton-Western Town, a difficult shoot demanding
many camera set-ups, as the scene to be filmed depicted the final battle
between the townspeople and the invading villains.

Looking over this schedule you will see that the low-budget film must
shoot quickly and economically. Sync sound was used only once during
the entire day, as all the fight scenes were shot MOS (without sound). We
added two Eymo combat cameras for some of the shoot-out scenes and
for the car roll, and Convict's charge through Main Street. The day's
shooting was complicated by intermittent rain, which forced the director
to change some of the set-ups, and to consolidate others.

Title Frozen Scream	Seq. # 3 Page # 2

Name of Location   Dr. Smith residence,   Day   xx   Night   x

Address 1203 Day Drive, Westlake   Phone   Contact Dr. Marvin Smith

Scene Number and Synopsis	Total Script Pages
6	Tom Gerard talks to Ann, he rummages through his desk.
Interior Gerard's residence. Study.	

Sound: SYNC

Cast and Wardrobe	Bits and Atmosphere
Tom—worn leather jacket brown sport slacks	none
	Props
	telephone
	lamp
	books on desk
	papers on desk
Special Equipt. & Const.	
	Cars Livestock Special Effects
	SOUND EFFECTS: Humming voices

Title **Frozen Scream**	Seq. # 2	Page # 1

Name of Location **Joe's Shell Station**   Day xx   Night x

Address **203 Elm Road, Hollywood**   Phone   Contact

Scene Number and Synopsis	Total Script Pages
2 **Interior car.**	**Ann driving**

Sound: **SYNC**

Cast and Wardrobe	Bits and Atmosphere
Ann—trench coat scarf	**none**

	Props
	Ann's purse

Special Equipt. & Const. Fog machine	
	Cars Livestock Special Effects **Ann's car**

Title Frozen Scream	Seq. # 1 Page # 1

Name of Location   Joe's Shell Station   Day   xx   Night   x

Address   203 Elm Road, Hollywood   Phone   Contact   Joe Miller

Scene Number and Synopsis	Total Script Pages 3/4
1	Ann's car approaches
2	Ann's car pulls into service station, and Ann walks towards telephone booth
Exterior, Service Station	

Sound: SYNC

Cast and Wardrobe	Bits and Atmosphere
Ann—trench coat, scraf	none

Props

Ann's purse

Special Equipt. & Const.

Fog machines

Cars Livestock Special Effects

Ann's car

109

Title Frozen Scream	Seq. # Page # 2

Name of Location Joe's Shell Station	Day xx Night x

Address 203 Elm Road   Phone   Contact Joe Miller

Scene Number and Synopsis	Total Script Pages 1/2

5

Interior telephone booth at service station

Ann searches for coin, dials.

Ann talks to Tom on phone

Sound: SYNC

Cast and Wardrobe	Bits and Atmosphere
Ann—trench coat scarf	none

Props

Ann's purse

coin

Special Equipt. & Const.

Fog machines

Cars Livestock Special Effects

HELL RIDERS.

COLTON WESTERN TOWN

8:00		*Crew Call*
8:00		*Make-up Call*
8:30	341	Low Angle—Stubby to jail—Bike
	344	Stubby falls back—shot
9:00	347	Rocky runs in, checks on Stubby
	349	Rocky falls
9:30	348	Locals fire—Dave (stops and leaves) —Sheriff fires
	350	Joe fires
	360	Chuck and Clyde fire
10:00	355	Convict fires—is hit, leaves
	352	Chuck falls (have tarp ready)
	354	Main Street—Sheriff hit
10:30	354A	Dave leaves building
	356A	Dave fires at Convict
	357	Dancer fires
	359	Dancer hit
	361	Dancer dying
11:00	357A	Dave hit, falls
	Roof	
12:00	340	Chuck up on roof, Dave motions him down
	341	Stubby runs to jail
	344	Stubby falls back
	347	Rocky runs in
	349	Rocky falls
	351	Convict and Chuck fight, falls
	353	Convict aims
1:00		*Lunch*
2:00		*Mainstreet*
	364	Claire walks to Dave's office Iris, Ella, Suzy, Harriet, Betsy walk to diner
		Joe & Clyde—(sync sound) dialogue
2:30	367	Convict starts car, stops at head of street, charges as girls fire
	372	Townspeople POV of car—traveling shot
	373	Interior Convict's car—His POV of street
	375	Convict yells
	377	Convict is hit (through glass)
	377A	Car turns
3:00	366	Dave wounded (special make-up), rises up, Claire picks up gun
	376	Claire fires at Convict's car
	376A	Car turns (POV Convict)
4:30		*Wrap*

111

CALL SHEET
CIARA PRODUCTIONS

Location _____   Call Time _____

Address _____   At _____

Phone _____   Date _____

Category	Name and Phone #	Time In	Time Out
Producer			
Director			
Prod. Mgr.			
P.A.			
Script			
Camera			
A.C.			
2nd Cam.			
Make-up			
Ast. Make-up			
Mixer			
Boom			
Gaffer			
Best Boy			
Electrician			
Slate			
Props			
Key Grip			
No 2			
Sets			
Driver			

Call: _____ First Shot: _____ Lunch _____

Wrapped _____ Exposed footage _____

Talent Name and Phone # _____ Agent Name and Phone # _____

1.

2.

3.

4.

5.

6.

Chapter Nine
Your Equipment

Filmmaking is an exciting creative activity once you have mastered the craft of lighting, sound work and photography. Few producers are masters in these arts. They have to rely on the expertise of the lighting director and sound man. "So why," you may ask, "do I need an entire chapter on equipment and its uses?" You won't be handling the camera, the Nagra, and the lights, but you should know about each and every piece of equipment to be used during the production. Chances are you will end up with a truckload full of unnecessary things if you are not thoroughly familiar with the logistics of the equipment required.

If you live in one of the filmmaking centers such as Hollywood or New York you will have a wide array of places renting cameras, as well as sound and grip equipment. Usually, no warranty of performance is given, though you should not pay for defective equipment. Make it a rule to check out the equipment at the time of pick-up. You *must* check out the camera, unless you don't mind losing hours of shooting time while the camera has to be exchanged. Let your cinematographer or his assistant make this check. Do not rely on the salesman's assurances.

Most low-budget film production companies rent their equipment on weekends. This way they pay a flat fee which is slightly higher than the one day fee, but they have their equipment for two days or better. Usually, you can arrange to pick up your equipment on Friday afternoon, shortly before closing time. The prudent producer will schedule either a night shoot or an interior shoot for Friday. Working about six hours on Friday night gives him about half an additional day. And believe me, these additional half days mount up.

Most equipment rental houses carry their own insurance. You will pay an additional ten percent of the rental fee for insurance. If you are renting very expensive equipment such as a BL camera which has a replacement cost of over $100,000, you are required to supply your own insurance. This insurance will cost you about $500 for four weeks.

Equipment must be returned before 10 a.m. the following day (for weekend rentals, on Monday), or you will have to pay for an additional day. Before returning your equipment, check it out again. Unfortunately, some rental houses have been known to charge you for non-existing "damages" or "losses."

All the large rental houses have catalogues. Often, you can get a better price by negotiating. If you have a shooting schedule of more than one week, you should get a considerable discount.

Camera

The heart of all your equipment is your camera. Test it out before you rent it. Beware. Watch out for *camera scratches* and *light leaks*. Run a small amount of film through the camera and the magazines and have it developed. Remember, the low-budget film production company cannot afford to lose any footage or time.

If part of the image on the screen is blurred, the camera shutter may be out of synchronization with the pull-down claw. If frames alternately go in and out of focus, then the film is "breathing" and you have a faulty pressure plate to deal with. All these defects must be repaired by an expert.

The first and most important consideration in choosing a camera is quality, and secondly the specifics of the film you are making. Frequently, different cameras are used for different parts of a film.

The standard camera of the 35mm theatrical industry is the Mitchell BNC. It runs silently, has a variable shutter, provisions for interchangeable motors and lenses, registration pins which hold each frame steady during exposure, and a wide array of accessories. The Mitchell is probably the very best camera you can rent, but it is very expensive, requires a fully professional crew, and is heavy and cumbersome.

A great favorite for low-budget production films is the Arriflex 35BL. This camera shoots silently, has variable shutters, interchangeable motors, and variable running speeds. Above all, it can be used hand-held, and runs from a battery pack. It is not inexpensive to rent, but will serve you well.

There are various models of Bell and Howell cameras available. Usually, the old "Eymo" combat camera (it does not run silently) is used as a second and third position camera during the shooting of action and stunt scenes. The "Eymo" takes 100-foot loads of film.

If you are not shooting sync sound (sound recorded on location with picture), and have decided to "loop" your sound later on during post-production, then you may consider either an Arriflex or a Bell and Howell. Both cameras are of excellent quality, sturdy, but comparatively lightweight. Both run from battery packs and can be hand held.

There are various models of 16mm cameras available. First of all, there is the Arriflex 16BL. Like the 35BL, it is a silent-running camera equipped with the same features as the 35BL. You may also consider:

Arriflex 16SH High Speed Camera
CP-16R Camera and 16RA Camera
Eclair ACL Camera
Bolex REX Camera (100' load)
Bolex REX V Camera (400' load)

Besides the lenses which we will discuss in the next segment, you will need the following accessories with your camera:

Magazines
Motors
Battery and power supply
Tripod and fluidhead
Dolly and tracks
Braces
Light meter

Each of these accessories—mandatory to shooting—will cost you separately. Adding these amounts to the cost of a variety of lenses means that you will have to spend a considerable amount of your budget on the *camera package*. At times, you will be able to hire a cinematographer who brings in his own camera for considerably less than you would pay at the rental houses. This may be a good deal, but make certain that the camera offered is of top quality. Do not hesitate to have it checked out for the previously mentioned defects. Also consider that few feature films are shot with only one camera. You will probably have to rent some additional cameras anyway.

Lenses

Using a variety of lenses in making a film will help you to get exciting footage. Since we are dealing with many different types of lenses, but have only a limited amount of space within the scope of this book, let's take a look at the most widely-used ones.

Lenses are identified by their *focal lengths*, expressed in millimeters. The focal length indicates the area a lens can photograph from a given point to the camera. The longer the focal length (the higher the number), the smaller the area the lens can photograph. The faster and sharper the lens, the more expensive it will be. Lenses for the 35mm camera are available from 14mm wide-angle to 250mm telephoto. The normal lens gauge is considered 50mm. For the 16mm camera, the range of lens choices is very similar to that of the 35mm camera.

The Normal Lens
A lens is considered normal if it yields an image of natural perspective, that is, the size of objects diminishes as their distance to the camera becomes greater. Remember, while perspective is controlled by the distance between the subject and the camera, it is only indirectly true that perspective is controlled by the focal length of the lens. In order to keep the subject at the same size as you move the camera closer or farther from it, you will have to change the focal length of your lens. If you use a longer lens, you will keep your subject in its original size, but you will have to change the perspective—objects farther away will not appear as small as they normally would. Since there is a compression of depth, your moving subject may seem to stand still. Using a wide-angle lens, the

opposite happens. As we exaggerate the perspective, the distance between foreground and background seems greater than it is in actuality.

The normal lens should be used only for intermediate filming distances. It is never a good idea to use a normal lense for close-ups. To film a pleasing close-up of a face, a lense of about 50% greater focal length is necessary to achieve normal perspective. Generally, it is better to use a lens of greater focal length while moving the camera farther away from the subject.

True perspective will vary every time subject-camera distances change, but these variations will not be noticed by your audience.

The Telephoto Lens

The telephoto lens has a much greater focal length than the normal lens and we will get an image much larger than the subject photographed with a normal lens. At the same time, we will get a much narrower-angle view. The more powerful the lens, the more the image is enlarged, and the more any jiggle of the camera is magnified. A telephoto lens will be a poor choice for any hand held camera work. Choosing a telephoto lens, you should select one that will show some distance behind your subject in acceptable sharp focus. This area of sharp focus is called the "depth of field," and is an important consideration in using the right telephoto lens.

Wide-Angle Lens

The wide-angle lens has a much greater depth of field than the normal or telephoto lens. Action can often be filmed without any need to focus during the shot. It allows for some very interesting compositions. A wide-angle lens allows you to get very close to your subjects and still maintain an overview look. The wide-angle lens produces a smaller image of a given subject at a given distance than does a normal lens. Therefore, you will find yourself shooting quite close. The use of a wide-angle lens reduces camera jiggles by the percentage that its focal length is shorter than the normal lens. You can see that the wide-angle lens is the perfect choice for:

Hand-held cameras
Dolly or tracking shots
Shots to be taken inside a moving vehicle

The Zoom Lens

A zoom lens can be considered a variable focal length lens. Often, zoom lenses are used at single settings. If you use the zoom lens in lieu of a camera tracking shot it will save you lots of time and effort. You will get your best effects for such simulated tracking shots if your shots require little depth of the field.

Lenses are important considerations not only as far as perspective and focal sharpness is concerned, but even more as you decide about the pictorial statement you wish to make. Many an interesting idea and a well designed storyboard has been ruined by the wrong lens. To illustrate this, let's quickly discuss a simple action shot. Your hero has to deliver a punch to the villain's face. The camera is set up from the villain's POV, featuring the hero in a MEDIUM SHOT.

The normal lens will result in a pictorial statement of medium interest. The audience will watch the punch without being involved.

The telephoto lens weakens the impact of the punch even more.

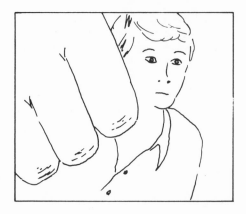

The wide angle lens (if you are close enough) will give you the desired effect. You will attack the viewer and as such you will force him to participate in the action.

Now let's take a look at the different lenses as we film a party scene celebrating our heroine's "Sweet 16" birthday. She is cutting the cake while her friends are gathered behind her.

- The normal lens will make no definite pictorial statement, but will help you to tell the story in a clear and effective manner.
- The telephoto lens will bring her friends (the background) much closer. Their presence will be more important than the heroine's. If you wish to tell us that she is unimportant to them, then you've got the right lens.
- The same scene shot with a wide-angle lens will make her friends seem distant and rather vague. This shot tells us she is stepping away from everything she has known and into a world of her own reality.

Unfortunately, this segment was able to give you but a short introduction to lenses. A number of excellent books have been published on cinematography, and deal with lenses in depth.

Filters

Working in color you will have many occasions to use filters. Filters will be screwed on the lens with the aid of an adapter ring. If your camera has a matte box you will be able to use less expensive gelatin filters. A filter in a matte box will cover any lens, regardless of its size. Since the focus of your lens changes slightly as you use a filter, your filters should be of high quality. Filters absorb light, and you must compensate in your exposure for this decrease in light. The filter factor (suggested by the manufacturer) represents the number of times the normal exposure must be increased. A filter factor of two means an increase of one whole F/stop.

Neutral Density Filter

The neutral density filter is a gray filter which cuts down the amount of light hitting the lens. It is used for high-speed film in bright light.

Polarizing Filter

A polarizing filter works only with polarized light, (sunlight or reflections on glass and water). It is used to darken the sky without changing the other colors on the film. It is a good way to shoot "day for night"— to shoot a "nighttime" scene during daylight. This filter will only work with sunlight, and for best results you need an effective interplay between light and shadows. Using the polarizing filter you will get a bright moonlight effect.

Diffusion Filter

A diffusion filter softens hard lines. It is frequently used for close-ups.

Fog Filter

A fog filter creates a fog effect by decreasing image definition. For best results you may do well to shoot preliminary tests.

Color Compensation Filter

A "skylight" filter can be used to tone down blue on snow. Another filter (Kodak #82) may be used to avoid a slightly red cast that at times occurs depending on the lighting set-up employed for interior shots. The same filter is helpful if you have to use lights during a daytime, outdoor shot.

The Camera Package

You have recognized the importance, and also the expense, of the "camera package." The low-budget producer has a multiplicity of problems and solutions to consider before he settles on the camera to be used. The basic questions to be answered are: "Will we shoot sync sound, or will we shoot MOS* and loop later?"

In sync sound, the camera and the Nagra (sound recorder) will work in synchronization. While this way of shooting is the only acceptable way for most low-budget films, and a major production would not even consider any other method of working, I feel it stands some scrutiny. The traditional way of doing things is not always the most expeditious one. Since low-budget film producers are normally strapped for money, they may do well to save some on their camera package. Let's consider the pros and cons of both sync sound and MOS.

*MOS pertains to "motion without sound."

119

Sync sound: On the positive side of the ledger we will find:

Dialogue will be very immediate and will have the quality of
realism.
Most distributors expect sync sound.

On the negative side of the ledger you will find:

The silent BL camera, mandatory for sync sound shooting, is
expensive.
It will take just as long to set up your sound equipment as it will take
to set up your lights and camera. Remember, the camera and
sound recorder must run in synchronization.
You may lose otherwise very acceptable shots because of either
sound/camera malfunction or overhead noise.
Your expense in raw stock and lab cost will go up due to these faulty
shots.

MOS: On the positive side of the ledger you will find:

You will save a very considerable amount of time and money, as you
will be able to use each acceptable take. The rental cost of the
camera is considerably less.

On the negative side of the ledger you will find:

Your sound is never as acceptable as with sync sound.
Many distributors will shy away from a looped film, stating that these
films all have a foreign feeling to them.
It is often very expensive to loop.
The looped sound never achieves the naturalness of the sync sound.
Often actors' deliveries become stilted as they have to lip sync. A
scene which has force and believability might lose much of its
impact once it is looped.

On some of my films I used sync sound, on others I had to loop the
dialogue. Generally, I encountered all the pros and cons listed above,
and finally came to the conclusion that the low-budget film producer
should combine sync sound and MOS. During the last rewrite of your
script be fully aware of your sound problems. Doctor your script in such
a way that all dialogue scenes will take place—indoors either in the
studio you have rented, or if on location, in a highly controllable area.
For these scenes, you will rent the sync sound camera and all necessary
sound equipment. Make certain that your actors know their lines before
shooting. At times it pays to hire a dialogue coach for your sound days.
The moment you shoot action scenes, or any outdoor scene for that
matter, shoot MOS. Of course, you have made certain in your script that
at this point the dialogue has been cut down to a bare minimum by
avoiding long, ponderous speeches. Make certain that sound effects

(chirping birds, traffic sounds, music, etc) will cover your "crime" of shooting MOS, and not even the most picky distributor will be aware of your having strayed away from the demanded sync sound.

If you have a good sound editor you will be saving even more money during post-production by avoiding lip sync looping. Have your actors go through their speeches, then cut loops. A skilled sound editor should have no difficulty adjusting the loops to the actor's lip movements. You will have to pay your editor more, but you will save on high sound lab cost.

The Sound Package

Nagra

The most convenient sound recorder to use is the Nagra recorder. The Nagra can be fitted with an oscillator identical to the unit controlling the camera speed. The tape running speed is recorded along the edge of the sound tape and thus provides a precise timing reference for the sound editor. There is no mechanical or electrical connection between the camera and the recorder. Both can be used physically independent of each other. Another method of sync sound recording is combining a camera with an internal sync pulse generator. This sync pulse is part of the motor. The output is fed through a wire to the tape recorder. The sound recording now contains the exact record of the camera running speed. At times, this method of sound recording inhibits the physical movability of the camera and the sound recorder.

When a sync sound film is being edited, the camera takes have to be lined up with their corresponding sound tracks. For this purpose start marks must be taken, or in filmmaking terms, "the film must be slated." Once the camera and the recorder are rolling, a slate giving the scene number is placed in front of the camera. A piece of wood is hinged on the top of the slate. The slate person reads out the information given on the slate, such as "Scene 302, Take One," then claps down the board. Later on the editor will line up the "clap" on the sound track with the picture frame in which the board hit the top of the slate.

Before and during recording, the sound should be monitored with a good headset. The headset is an important feature. It cuts out background sounds. Since headsets are usually stereo, you need an adapter plug to convert them to monaural.

Overmodulating (over-recording) occurs when the tape is overloading, and distortions will result. All recorders have some provisions to indicate overmodulating. When the meter does not move, you are either not recording at all, or the sound that you are recording is too low. When the meter moves to +8db you are overloading. Normal speech should be recorded between -18 and -8 db. To avoid over or under recording, the soundman should anticipate volume changes.

When recording out of doors, you may pick up wind noise. An in-line filter or windscreen behind your microphone cuts out the static-type wind noise. In an emergency you may either pull a nylon sock over the microphone or wrap it in acoustic foam.

Microphones
If you demand acceptable sound, you need a variety of microphones even for a low-budget film.

General Purpose Directional Microphone
A directional mike gives excellent sound if placed in front of your actors, but is unresponsive if the sound comes from any other direction. It is used primarily for two-shots. The directional mike can very easily be hidden behind a flower pot, some books or other objects. The recorded sound has presence.

Omnidirectional Microphone
If your actors are sitting opposite each other, you will need the omnidirectional mike. This mike picks up sounds from all directions. Using this mike, you will have to sacrifice some sound presence and background noise rejection.

Shotgun Microphone
This mike is a highly directional mike, and it does not produce sound of as good a quality as the general purpose directional mike. It should not be used for close range recording. It is used primarily as a special problem solver.

Lavalier Microphone
The Lavalier is a tiny mike concealed under the lapels of an actor's jacket or in the neckline of your leading lady. The cables coming from these mikes run into a volume control box called the mixer. The mixer output is then fed into the recorder. Lavalier mikes have a tendency to hamper the actor's movement to an uncomfortable degree.

Boom
In many instances the boom man has to follow the conversation of two or more people. The microphone is mounted on a boom, or fishpole, which dangles over the actors' heads. The boom man has to be very skilled to avoid boom shadows on the film. He also must be able to anticipate when each actor is going to speak. This represents an added difficulty—each involuntary move of the aluminum pole, the fishpole, in his hand will be recorded as an unpleasant rasping sound.

In the previous segment I mentioned the danger of camera noise, and the high expense of renting a silent camera. If you are faced with the problem of having to use a noisy camera, you should use a directional mike close to your actors, then place the camera a good distance away and use a telephoto lens. As an added precaution, you should wrap your camera in a nylon-quilted or feather-filled ski jacket.

The Lighting Package

In a low-budget film production, the lighting is usually considered the responsibility of the cinematographer. I would suggest turning this responsibility over to the gaffer. There are a million things the cameraman has to consider and worry about, and it is better to give this important responsibility to two people. Both cinematographer and gaffer should decide on the lighting in concert, but it is the gaffer who actually sets the lights. Light is one of the elements that determines the mood of the picture. Lighting helps in telling the story you want to create on the screen. Often it is a primary part of the story, and for this reason you would design a different lighting plot for a horror film than you would for an action or relationship picture. In short, your story determines your lighting.

Types of Lighting Equipment

There is a wide variety of lighting fixtures at your disposal. The three most useful types of lights for low-budget film productions are tungsten halogen lights, photofloods and reflectors.

Photofloods are similar to household bulbs, but run on a much higher voltage and for this reason have a much shorter life span. They come in wattages from 200 to 1000. You will be able to use photofloods between two and six hours. They are ideal for interior shooting, as they have a very bright light output.

Reflector type lights come in spot (highly concentrated beam) and flood (less concentrated beam) lights. One of the best light kits on the market is the Lowell-Light set. It is usually fairly inexpensive to rent, and is lightweight and adjustable to many uses.

Halogen lights are the most versatile of all the tungsten (quartz—iodine) lights. They keep a constant color temperature, and have a long life span. Halogen lights require only a small, lightweight housing, and you can change the light from spot to flood position. However, the quartz bulbs are fairly expensive. Halogen lights come with a number of very useful accessories:

Dichroic daylight conversion filters to change the light to the same color temperature as the daylight.
Heat filters to cut down the heat generated by the bulb.
Intensifier skirts to increase the light output.
Scrims to diffuse the intensity of the light.

Soft lights are excellent for lighting a large area with a minimum of shadow. The Colortran Soft Light unit is available in wattages from 750 to 4000.

Sun-guns are useful for situations where you are unable to plug into light sources or use a generator because of its inconvenient bulk. Sylvania makes a battery-powered unit that will last about thirty minutes before it needs recharging. The battery can be worn on a belt and the unit is hand held. The light is rather flat and does not lend itself to interesting shadow effects. Sun guns should only be used as a last resource.

Faced with the wide variety of lights and accessories, it is as easy for the low-budget producer to go overboard on his lighting package as it is to skimp. Generally speaking, you should not have more lighting equipment than can be handled by your lighting crew. Often, productions slow down because of the unrealistic amount of equipment to be used. On the other hand, you should not find yourself without sufficient equipment. Ideally, you should have enough lighting to work on one location while the lighting crew sets up the next one. It is difficult to suggest a basic lighting package, since each production differs in many ways. Still, this is my suggestion:

Lowell-Light set
Four photofloods
Four soft lights
Two halogen lights

Lighting Accessories

You will need a number of accessories with your lamps:

Tripod lighting stand
Sandbags to hold tripod in place
Aluminum reflectors
Scrims
Barndoors (to shape the light beam)
Silks (to diffuse lights)
Cables
Flags (to create interesting shadows)
Gels
Clamps
Gaffer's tape
Generator (if no electricity is available, such as during exterior shooting at night)

The Basic Light Set-Up

Your lighting director and your gaffer are artists as well as craftsmen. Naturally, they (the same as you) want the most artistic and best light plot possible. Setting lights is time consuming, and unfortunately, time is of the essence in low-budget filmmaking. Often you have to make do. The distribution of light (disregarding the artistic purpose) has to "model" the subjects on the screen. People and objects should give us the illusion of a three-dimensional appearance.

Key light: The key light is the main light illuminating and "modeling" the subject. This is the light that most likely will determine the F/stop to be used. It should remain consistent throughout the scene. If the key light is a spot, you will have to contend with strong, at times dramatic, at other times unflattering shadows. If it is a flood it will give a rather uninteresting and flat appearance.

Fill light: The key light (or key lights) always require fill lights. The fill light is usually placed near the camera, on the side opposite the key light, and is used to lighten shadows. It is half as bright as the key light.

Back light: The back light is a very bright spot placed behind the subject. It will help to create a feeling of depth to the composition.

Front light: Front light is any light from the camera position to the subject. This lighting gives a flat and often harsh effect. It tends to give razor sharp shadows.

Side light and top light come from the side and top of the subjects position.

Low key lighting is used to heighten suspense. Everything is in shadow, a few highlights barely define the subject.

High key lighting has few shadows, and tends to give a bright, everyday feel to set and subjects.

Rim lighting illuminates a subject from right to left. The lighting units are placed well back, behind the subject, so that only the edge of the figure shows illumination.

Some Helpful Hints

Of course, there is no formula for lighting any scene since so many variables have to be considered. What is the mood you wish to establish, how much time you have to set the lights, will your camera be static or will it move, are just a few of the considerations your lighting director has to struggle with.

Generally, it is best to place the lighting units high off the floor. Such placement creates flattering shadow patterns—it highlights the cheekbones and models the actors' faces. If the lights are high up, they will not be in the camera's field of view, and will permit the camera to move more freely.

For the low-budget film production it is always advantageous to work with one general lighting set-up for each scene, adding or subtracting fill lights and back lights as the situation demands. It is wise to discuss the various lighting plots with your lighting director during the storyboard stage of your film. You will find out that you will have to modify a number of scenes in order to eliminate additional lighting set-ups. Remember, changing lights is time consuming, and time is money in the low-budget film production.

One of the main problems the cinematographer encounters as he moves his camera is either light fixtures or unwanted shadows in his field of view. At times, he feels confronted with an impossible situation, as he has to shoot an action scene taking place within a wide area. Let's assume he has to shoot a stalk scene in an underground garage. Unfortunately, he has to shoot a master shot, and for this reason has to light the entire garage. Setting up lights on high angles would take the better part of the day, and is out of the question. You will simply *area light* the garage, leaving parts dark, while placing your lighting units behind crates, parked cars, columns and the like. At other times, you will be able to put your lights right in the shot, and still not draw attention to them. Large spot-lights at the scene of an accident, or photo floods in a photographer's studio will look quite plausible to your audience.

Hallways seem to present a difficulty, even though these areas are fairly easy to light. All you have to do is open a few doors, place lights behind them, and aim the light out into the hallway.

Another difficulty are scenes taking place in the "dark." Naturally, you wish to light the scene in such a way as to give the illusion of darkness and still show your audience what is going on. The secret is to use rim lighting only. The outlines of your actors will be noticeable against the dark background, but the scene will give the impression of taking place totally in the dark. Usually you will light your actor from right to left, with the lights placed well behind him. In a close-up you will provide somewhat more light by setting the illumination level on the face in such a way that there is only 25 percent of normal exposure.

When photographing the close-up of your female star, be careful to provide for silks over the lights. Harsh lighting will be unflattering to even the youngest and prettiest face. You should also take into consideration that heavy make-up tends to age any face in light. Therefore, make-up should be applied sparingly and lightly.

Daytime exterior filming will also bring its measure of difficulties to overcome. Now you will have to contend with frequent light changes. You may film your actors in a medium shot while the sun shines brightly. A little while later as you do the close-ups for the reversal shots, the sunshine has either diminished or increased in intensity. If there is now less sunshine than before you must use your reflectors to increase the light available to you, and to recreate the same effect of light and shadows that you had before. If the light is brighter than it was previously, you have to use tarps to shade your scene.

Chapter Ten

The Final Phase of Pre-production

One of the most important responsibilities of the low-budget, independent producer is to consider each detail of his project. He has to decide about each miniscule part of the film to be produced, he has to take into consideration each and every eventuality that may arise. Believe me, the success of his film hinges on his ability to think things through.

About fourteen days before the start of principal photography, it is his task to tie up the loose ends. He will breathe a sigh of relief realizing that: "The major disasters are behind me. Once principal photography starts I have only to deal with minor ones." Then he will roll up his sleeves as he gets ready to tackle last minute emergencies such as:

Final Budget
Insurance
Permits
Crew
Catering

Final Budget

During this last phase of pre-production it is mandatory to go through the budget once more, and hopefully for the last time. I know, we all review the budget with a sense of trepidation but nevertheless, review it we must. It's likely there won't be many changes. All costs, including the salaries of the yet unhired crew, will remain fairly static. Still you may give your financial approach to the production some second thoughts. Many producers, in their eagerness to get the film on the road sell themselves short financially. It is now the time to ask yourself, "Is it possible to bring in the film on budget, or is there any chance I will go over budget?" In most cases, you may see there is a good chance of going over budget since there are some eventualities, like rain or equipment failure, you have not considered. You need a contingency fund, a certain amount of money which you will not touch. Unfortunately, your meager budget consists of bare-bones necessities only, even more unfortunately it is now too late to ask for more money. You have to squeeze your contingency fund out of your sickly budget. There is no other way.

Still, you'll have to cut down somewhere. But, let me warn you, do not cut down on the stars you've hired or on the effects (stunts or special effects) you have promised to deliver. The distributor depends on these selling points. They are the "cherries on top of the sundae" that he presents to the buyers. There are only two areas you can cut down—shooting days and locations.

I doubt whether it is wise for the average low-budget film producer to cut down on shooting time. Usually you will not have more than fourteen days at your disposal anyway. However, if your budget calls for a three-week shoot, then you may easily snip off two days. Your savings will be considerable.

The most likely area where you can save falls within the location budget. A sizable hunk can be cut from the total production costs by simply considering:

1. A night scene might be changed to a day scene, or it may be shot "day for night." In this event, the savings in equipment and set-up time will be considerable.
2. A setting might be revamped to serve double duty.
3. An outdoor scene might be shot indoors, or vice versa.
4. An inexpensive location might be substituted for a more expensive one.
5. A location fairly close by may be substituted for one requiring extensive travel. In this case you will not only save on per diem, but also on wear and tear on the cast and the crew.
6. A dialogue taking place in a driving car can be changed to a stationary location. In this case you will save on equipment (camera mounts) and set-up time.
7. A shootout taking place on the staircase of a high-rise office building might be consolidated to something less demanding. In this instance you will save set-up time if you start the shootout on the staircase, but let it take place on the roof of the building. Staircase set-ups are difficult and time consuming. Things move much faster on the even surface of the roof.
8. Do you need two separate set-ups for your storyline, or is it possible to substitute sound for one set up? In "Frozen Scream," the heroine was caught in the building which the villain entered by breaking a window. Frank Roach, the director, consolidated these scenes ingeniously by focusing on the heroine's reaction as she heard glass shatter.
9. Do you need the big party scene, or will a few dancing couples, cleverly staged behind your stars, *suggest* an elaborate party?
10. Remember the low-budget production creed, "If in doubt, shoot tight medium," and ask yourself if possibly the four corners of a room (dressed appropriately) might make for more economic shooting than dragging the equipment from room to room throughout the house.
11. Could you possibly shoot your car chases and stunts on the expensive location, and later add all dialogue, hiring a less expensive place. You'll have to decide whether the savings are considerable enough to justify an added day.

Of course, your decisions cannot be based on budgetary considerations alone. You should always keep the artistic statement of your film in mind. Sometimes the budget and sometimes the artistic statement will win out in your final decision. However, it is you the producer who has to make this decision. It is your obligation to bring in the film on the agreed upon budget. Do not let anyone change your mind, may he or she be the director, the cinematographer, or your tennis partner. If you are cutting some things out, *they must remain cut.* Do not permit anyone to doubt the fact that you are in charge of the production and the final authority in all decisions to be made.

Insurance

You do need insurance, there is no doubt about it. Without insurance you will not be given any permits. I always carry these insurance policies:

Liability (one million)
Workmen's compensation
Rented vehicle insurance (if I use stunt cars)
Equipment insurance (including camera insurance)

It is better to buy your liability and workmen's compensation insurance from your insurance broker, the one who handles your automobile and homeowner policies. You will get a better deal from him than you will from those insurance companies specializing in motion picture insurance. You should buy your insurance for a full year, not only for the duration of principal photography. The cost is slightly higher but well worth the investment.

However, you should buy your equipment and rented vehicle insurance from a motion picture insurance company. They are the only ones handling these types of policies. Buy your insurance for the duration of principal photography *only.* You may also buy *negative insurance* in case your negative gets destroyed.

Another type of insurance, the *completion bond,* is very expensive and is issued by firms specializing in completion bonds.

Permits

If you intend to shoot either in Los Angeles or New York, *you do need permits.* It doesn't matter whether you plan to shoot in your Aunt Louisa's kitchen or on the main thoroughfare in Griffith Park. You do need a permit. Shooting within the city limits, you will receive your permits from the city. If you plan to go outside the city area, you'll have to contact the county to get your permit. Both cities are equally stringent in their requirements, which—naturally—has forced many bigger and smaller companies to take their location money to other, more cooperative counties, and states, and even countries. The stringent permit conditions are partially to blame for the exodus to "greener" pastures. Nevertheless, I found the officials working for both Los Angeles City and County friendly, helpful, and always ready with good advice.

It is best to mail Xerox copies of your liability and workmen's compensation insurance to the city or county film commission. About a week to ten days prior to your shooting at a specific location, you request a permit to be issued. This request should be made by phone. In case you intend to film on either county or city property (such as a park) you have to get in touch with the agency in charge (Los Angeles Parks and Recreation Division in Los Angeles) to find out whether the location is available on the day requested.

The film office will reserve the location for you after you have informed them about:

Number of cars to be parked.
Number of people on the location, including cast and crew members.
Will there be any special effects, gunshots, car chases or stunts?
Will a generator be used?

If you are shooting at an exterior location, a fire marshall will be assigned to your company. It is wise to get the fire marshall's name and telephone number, in case you have to cancel a shoot. Should you not notify him about this cancellation ahead of time, you are obligated to pay his salary.

You may also have to pay for a water truck and a driver to be on the location. The cost for your permit is $135 and it is good for seven days. In the event that you wish to film on a number of locations, you will have to pay a rider of $20 for each.

Crew

The crew consists of a small army on the average studio and big independent production. You will have to do with a fraction of the people considered "essential" by your big competitors. Having a small crew is only a blessing in disguise. Contrary to popular opinion, the size of your crew does not make for quicker and better set-ups. It is the efficiency of the people that counts. The low-budget film producer cannot afford to hire amateurs. He must have experts for all areas requiring personnel. I have seen it over and over—a minimum of equipment along with a minimum of *expert* technicians can make for efficient and artistically acceptable filming.

You should listen to your director and your director of photography about any preferences they may have. It is always beneficial to a production if people have worked well together before, if they know and respect each other. However, you should never forget that it is you who

130

does the final hiring. In this respect you should take care not to permit the establishment of little empires (the director's people, the director of photography's people, and so on) or your own effectiveness as producer might be seriously hampered.

Now let's take a good look at the people you need on your crew:

Production Manager

I doubt seriously whether you really need the services of a production manager. He is the person who works on the budget, the breakdown and the shooting schedule during pre-production, all duties that you as producer have already fulfilled. On the shoot, the production manager is responsible for the day-to-day details such as getting permits, securing equipment and raw stock, and so on. Again, I feel he is unnecessary, as you will be on the shoot anyway and you will be the one to solve all upcoming problems. (However, if you are engaged in any other activity besides producing, such as directing or acting, you do need a production manager as soon as you go into principal photography.)

Naturally you will not get the permits or purchase props and incidentals. It is more efficient to hire a *production assistant* for these varied duties than to pay a production manager.

Production Assistant

The efficient production assistant is well on his way to becoming either a production manager or a producer. He will take the job because of the ample opportunities to learn. Basically, he will run errands, and so he needs a dependable car (the production company will pay for his considerable gas bills). He has to be a person of high dependability and integrity, as he is likely to be handling large amounts of cash. He is in charge of the petty cash, those incidental small purchases that are the bane of every low-budget film. Here the producer has to take a strong stand. Not one member of crew or cast is permitted to purchase *anything* without the producer's consent. The production assistant has to clear every purchase over $5 with the producer. I know this sounds niggardly, but purchases have a manner of escalating quickly if the producer fails to put on the brakes, and petty cash outlays can rip an embarrassing hole into your meager budget. On the shoot the P.A. will assist the art director, and will be in charge of the props.

Gaffer

The chief electrician is responsible, under the lighting director, for the lighting of the set. On most low-budget film productions, it is the lighting director who fulfills the gaffer's duties.

Best Boy

He is the gaffer's assistant. He should be an electrician. Since time is of the essence on a low-budget production, it's helpful to give the gaffer two assistants. During exterior shots they are responsible for the setting up of the reflectors.

Key Grip

The key grip is responsible for moving and setting up camera tracks, walls, flats, and so on. The key grip should have one assistant.

Mixer

The mixer is the senior member of the sound crew in charge of the dialogue or sound effects to be recorded. It is his responsibility to hand the recorded tape to the production manager or producer.

Boom Man

The boom man is the person who operates the boom that supports the microphone. He also is in charge of all microphones used during shooting.

Assistant Cameraman

Most likely your director of photography will not only be responsible for the movements and setting of the camera, but he will operate the camera as well. His assistant cameraman will pull focus and will carry out all the adjustments demanded by the director of photography. At times, he will operate the camera. He is also responsible for the daily camera report.

Loader

The loader will remove exposed film and reload the film magazines. He uses a light-proof, zippered bag in which the magazines are placed. It is constructed in such a way as to allow the loader to reach in without exposing the film to light. The loader should not be given any additional duties. Most low-budget films use the less expensive 300' to 400' rolls (short ends) and the loader will be fully occupied changing the magazines.

Slate

This is a position which might be filled by a grip. Operating the slate looks easy enough, but presents some difficulties for a newcomer. The slate is a pair of hinged boards giving information about scene numbers and date. The boards are clapped together in dialogue shooting as soon as picture and sound recorder are running at synchronized speed. It is important for the editor to be aware of the sync between sound and picture track, and therefore the "slate person" must be able to follow directions immediately and accurately.

Assistant Director (AD)

His title describes his duties completely. He has to assist the director in each and every way possible. On the low-budget production he has some added duties as well:

He will rehearse lines with the actors.
He will call, "Quiet on the set," before every take.
He is in charge of the call sheet.

He will notify the actors (and in the case of the low-budget film, also the crew) about their call times for the next day.

Script Supervisor

The script supervisor keeps all written records of all scenes and takes filmed. It is the script supervisor's responsibility to record:

Duration of scene.
Direction of movement.
Direction of looks.
Placement of actors and related props.
Notes from the director to the editor.

At the end of each shooting day the script supervisor should report to the producer, informing him about actual screen time filmed during the day. Often the script supervisor feels more obligated to the director than the producer, and is reluctant to give the needed information. From the first shooting day on, the producer should establish a good working relationship with the script supervisor.

Key Make-Up Artist

The key make-up artist should be well skilled in a wide variety of make-up assignments. Glamor make-up, horror make-up, scars, and open wounds are just a few of the demands he has to fill. It is wise to give the key make-up artist one assistant. For heavy make-up days a second assistant should be added. It saves not only time, but also wear and tear on everyone's nerves if the actors are in their positions at the designated time. The make-up crew should not be permitted to establish a comfortable "home base" away from the shoot, but they should be with everyone right in the trenches. It is the key make-up artist's responsibility to see that every actor and actress is powdered off before they go in front of camera, and that lipstick and general make-up is perfect. The actors should not be allowed to freshen their own make-up.

For the low-budget production, the assistant make-up artist is responsible for hair, and should be an experienced hairdresser.

The key make-up artist should bring his own make-up supplies. The production company will pay for any special make-up or special effects make-up required.

Wardrobe Mistress

For a picture rather undemanding as far as costumes are concerned, you may assign the duties of the wardrobe mistress to the assistant make-up artist. If a picture is more demanding in this area, you should hire a wardrobe person. The wardrobe person should also assist with props and any other duties required from a production assistant.

Catering

No matter how small your budget is, you should serve one hot meal per day. Of course you may prefer to buy lunch from any chicken or hamburger place, but you will save little in comparison to a catered meal. There are various catering services to choose from, and most likely you'll find a firm that "caters" to your budget. Before each shoot I let my crew and actors know that they will receive only one hot meal, and are responsible for their own breakfast and snacks.

I am opposed to the established custom of serving donuts and coffee in the morning. The quick sugar and starch intake makes people immediately tired and slows them down. I am also opposed to having "snacks and munchies" on the set, as well as soft drinks. These seemingly small items can be your budget killer. However, I do provide coffee, tea and lots of ice water during the days we film on dusty and hot exterior locations.

I never heard any complaints, as everyone brought their own thermos, fruit and some snacks.

Having a good meal catered is fun. Everyone seems to look forward to lunch, to rest and to share some laughs. I try to steer the caterer away from heavy fried and starchy foods. I also do not allow more than a 3/4-hour lunch break. The producer should be the last one going through the lunch line, and the first one to go back to work.

The Producer's Checklist

Last, but not least, the producer will write himself a little checklist to remind him of his rights and obligations.

Day Before the Shoot
- Confirm locations.
- Have any necessary equipment picked up (each department is responsible for picking up their own equipment).
- Pick up permits—production assistant.
- Pick up props—production assistant.
- Pick up wardrobe—wardrobe mistress.
- Call crew for call times—assistant director.
- Call actors for call times—assistant director.
- Go with the director through the shot list, and make adjustments if the schedule seems too heavy.
- Write out needed checks.

On the Shoot
Observe, but do not interfere. If you feel something needs to be corrected—such as too many takes, if director of photography and director seem out of sync, if an actor has not done his homework, or if set-ups are too slow—do not bear down on the offender with the wrath of

an ancient god, but unobtrusively take the director aside and correct the issue. Yes, the director is in charge once you are on the set, but let no one forget you are in charge of the entire production.

Take care of any emergencies, and there will be enough to keep you hopping. Do not permit anyone, star, actor or crew member to waste your time with idle chatting. Remain friendly, but aloof.

Wrap

• Check with director and script supervisor about being on schedule. How many minutes of actual screen time are in the can? What was the shooting ratio? Have we used too much raw stock? Have we filmed all the scenes listed on the shot sheet?

• Check with the assistant cameraman about the camera report. Each film can should be marked with a report, listing the footage of each scene shot, scene numbers, and what should be printed.

• Retain one copy of the report for your files. Assign someone, usually the production assistant, to take the film to the lab.

• Get the sound takes from the mixer, and have the production assistant take the tapes to the sound lab.

• Go through the call sheet with the assistant director and have him notify the crew and the cast about call times for the next day. Have him call actors not present on the set.

• Make certain that each department packs all their equipment.

• Discuss the next day's scenes with the director and the director of photography.

• Check out all petty cash envelopes brought in during the day. Jot all these details down in your daily production report.

As you can easily see, your most important task is to *keep the production on schedule.* This has to be done in an efficient, yet unobtrusive way. You cannot run around (as I have experienced) yelling, "We are behind schedule! Let's keep moving, people," but you should keep a keen eye on your shooting schedule. In case the director is about two hours behind schedule, it is your responsibility to consider the following alternatives:

1. Can the scene we are presently shooting be simplified to some extent?
2. If this should prove to be impossible, ask the director whether any of the following scenes might be simplified.
3. Could any of the scenes on today's shooting schedule be "scrapped?"
4. Is it possible to shoot establishing shots of all or any of the scheduled scenes, and to pick up the missing dialogue or details later? (This solution applies only if you are shooting on an expensive location.)
5. Are the difficulties caused by actors? What are the reasons for the difficulties.?

6. Are the difficulties because of equipment failure? Inclement weather?
7. Are the difficulties or delays caused by inefficient or slow set-ups?

The decision about getting back on schedule should be made in concert with the director. Chances are that you will be the one who has to make the final decision, and it is possible that you will meet with some resistance. Remain firm, do not give in to either star, director or cinematographer. Your decision (might it be right or wrong) stands, as you are the one who has to justify everything pertaining to the production.

Chapter Eleven
Post Production

After the last roll of film has been shot, the paper plates and champagne bottles from the "wrap party" have been cleared away, equipment, cameras and costumes have been returned, after actors and crew have gone their ways, only two lonely people—the producer and the director—remain on the empty battlefield. It is now that their motion picture moves into its third, and final phase—post-production. Post-production may take many months for the major studio film, but it should not take over three months for its low-budget competitor. One considers a motion picture "almost" finished after principal photography has commenced, yet it has to undergo a number of transformations until you and I will finally see it on the screen. Here are the steps:

Editing (picture and sound editing)
Sound (music and sound effects)
Answer print (negative cutting, titles, opticals, timing,
    final answer print)

Each step in itself is complicated and presents many decisions to be made. (Yes, you've guessed it, it is you as producer who has to make these decisions.)

Editing

Editing consists of the selecting and arranging of shots into sequences, and the arranging of sequences into a motion picture. It is editing that makes or breaks a film. There are many instances where a poor film was made acceptable by an excellent editor, and there are a few others where a good film was ruined by a less efficient editor. The good editor is not only a craftsman, but he is an artist in his own right. In some instances, if it is the director who edits, an editor and his staff usually join the production after principal photography has been completed. Producer, director, and editor must be in concert to give the film the desired look and rhythm.

The visual weight of each image contributes to the look of the film. Therefore each shot should have been filmed with a rhythm element in mind. Ideally, the director decided during the pre-production stage which scenes would require little editing and which ones need extensive work. The general rule of thumb is that violent action scenes require lots of coverage. The harshness of the sudden cuts helps to convey the emotional state of the characters. There are various points of contention in regards to editing, all pertaining to the dramatic statement to be conveyed. There are scenes that are best rendered by a few shots of long duration, and others by a number of short ones. Of course, when shots are held longer, camera movement will be more prominent. The balance between camera movement and editing, and the degree of editing within and between scenes is one of the determining factors of a film style. Editing should not be done to give a film "style" at any cost. But every cut, every camera movement should have significance, as audience attention should be directed to the dramatic purpose only. Editing should be logical. It should inform without being obvious. The audience should never become aware of the cutting. Unnecessary changes in angle and position should be avoided.

We can distinguish between four methods, or styles, of continuity editing:

Subjective
Point-of-View
Invisible
Emphatic

Subjective Editing
This is a style of editing that attempts to give the audience a notion on how things are being seen by the characters in the film. A sequence of three cuts is preceded by an establishing shot that tells the audience about the spatial relations between characters and things. Edited subjectively, the following scene from "FROZEN SCREAM" might look like this:

LONG SHOT: Tom on the phone. We take in the booklined study, his desk covered with papers, the telephone and the old clock on the wall.
MEDIUM SHOT: Tom, while talking to Ann, looks up.
CU: Tom's POV, the clock ticking away mercilessly.
TIGHT MEDIUM SHOT: Reluctantly, Tom puts down the receiver.
CU: Tom's POV, Ann's picture next to the telephone.
TIGHT MEDIUM SHOT: Tom hesitates for a moment, he opens a desk drawer, he hesitates again, then his hand grips an object.
TIGHT MEDIUM SHOT: Tom's hand as he pulls out the gun.

Point-Of-View Editing
This method dispenses with point-of-view shots, and consists of an establishing shot, medium shot and close-up. Our scene has changed in emotional and dramatic emphasis:

LONG SHOT: Tom on the phone. We establish the place and the time of the scene. He speaks into the telephone for a moment, looks up towards the clock, and the camera pulls in to a—

MEDIUM SHOT as he reluctantly puts down the receiver. He
hesitates for a beat, picks up Ann's picture, looks at it, then puts it
back next to the telephone. He opens the desk drawer, rummages
for an object—
CLOSE-UP: His hand gripping a gun, while we hear a SUDDEN
PIERCING ELECTRONIC SOUND.

You will notice that subjective editing creates a highly tense situation,
the audience *expects something to happen*, while in point-of-view editing
nothing is revealed until the audience is given shock information.

Invisible Editing

Invisible editing is functional, and establishes clear and logical
movements between points of space and time. It gives the audience a
sense of objective reality which makes them more viewers than partici-
pants. This type of editing is often keyed to movement within the scene.
G. W. Pabst was one of the strongest exponents of invisible editing. He
made every cut on some movement—on the end of one cut someone is
moving, at the beginning of the adjoining one the movement is contin-
ued. He stated, "The eye is thus so occupied in following these movements, that it misses the cuts." Invisible editing is often accompanied by
a shift of movement, following the logic within a scene. Using invisible
editing, we would start with Ann on the telephone:

EXT—TELEPHONE BOOTH—NIGHT
TIGHT MEDIUM SHOT: Ann smiles and *shakes her head*.

Cut To:

FULL SHOT
EXT—TOM GERARD'S HOUSE—NIGHT—V.O. ANN
The shadow of a man hurries around the corner, he *opens the door*
to the house.

Cut To:

MEDIUM SHOT
INT—TOM GERARD'S HOUSE/STUDY—NIGHT
While speaking on the phone to Ann he *moves his head* and looks
at the clock.

Cut to:

MEDIUM SHOT
EXT—TELEPHONE BOOTH—NIGHT
Softly smiling to herself, Ann *hangs up the receiver*.

Emphatic Editing

D. W. Griffith was the first director to employ this style of editing
which attempts the juxtaposition of strong patterns of rhythm, emphasis
and emotion. Emphatic editing relies on the emphatic use of close-ups. It

varies and accelerates cuts within the scene, and builds strong sequences by the use of cross-cutting (or parallel cutting). In this case, the director would start on Ann as she leaves the telephone booth:

EXT—TELEPHONE BOOTH—NIGHT
LONG SHOT: Ann leaves the telephone booth. Slowly she walks to her car. The car's headlights are islands of security in the fog engulfing Ann. (This shot is long and leisurely, depending on the actress's and the camera's movement.)

Cut To:

EXT—TOM GERARD'S HOUSE—NIGHT
A shadowy figure slips around the corner, it hesitates, looks up to the lighted window.

Cut To:

INT—TOM GERARD'S HOUSE/STUDY—NIGHT
MEDIUM SHOT: Tom sits very still as if frozen. He looks at the telephone. Finally he picks up Ann's picture.
CLOSE-UP: Ann's picture.
CLOSE-UP: On Tom, as he reacts to his wife's picture.

(You'll notice, both, the exterior and interior scenes are fairly leisurely in rhythm, but faster than the preceding long shot of Ann walking to her car.)

Cut To:

EXT—TOM GERARD'S HOUSE—NIGHT
MEDIUM SHOT: The shadowy figure walks to the door. He reaches out.
CLOSE-UP: His hand turning the door knob.

Cut To:

INT—TOM GERARD'S HOUSE/DEN—NIGHT
TIGHT MEDIUM SHOT: Tom looks at the clock.
CLOSE-UP: The clock. It ticks louder and louder.
TIGHT MEDIUM SHOT: On Tom, he pulls out the desk drawer.
CLOSE-UP: On Tom.

(The rhythm now becomes faster, it builds up even more speed as we add cross cutting.)

EXT—TELEPHONE BOOTH—NIGHT
CLOSE-UP: On car lights, camera pulls back as Ann approaches the car.
CLOSE-UP: Shock zoom—the car lights.

Cut To:

INT—TOM GERARD'S HOUSE/DEN—NIGHT
CLOSE-UP: On clock. It ticks unbearably loudly.
MEDIUM SHOT: Tom rummages through his desk drawer.

Cut To:

INT—TOM GERARD'S HOUSE/HALLWAY—NIGHT
CLOSE-UP: A hand closing the door firmly.

Cut To:

INT—TOM GERARD'S HOUSE/DEN—NIGHT
MEDIUM SHOT: Tom pulls out his gun, he listens.

Cut To:

EXT—TELEPHONE BOOTH—NIGHT
TIGHT MEDIUM: Quickly Ann enters the car, she slams the door shut

Cut To:

INT—TOM GERARD'S HOUSE/HALLWAY—NIGHT
CLOSE-UP: On feet walking through the hallway and up some steps.

Cut To:

EXT—TELEPHONE BOOTH—NIGHT
FULL SHOT: Car speeding away.

Cut To:

INT—TOM GERARD'S HOUSE/HALLWAY—NIGHT
CLOSE-UP: On feet going up stairs.

INT—TOM GERARD'S HOUSE/DEN—NIGHT
TIGHT MEDIUM SHOT: Tom gets up, he hears some sound.
CLOSE-UP: Tom's reaction.
INT—TOM GERARD'S HOUSE/HALLWAY—NIGHT
CLOSE-UP: On feet.

Cut To:

INT—TOM GERARD'S HOUSE/DEN—NIGHT
TIGHT CLOSE-UP: Tom listening.

Looking at these examples it should be clear that much of the
emotional statement depends on the editing. Still, it is the director who
will decide the coverage to be shot, and in this respect it is he who
controls editing. Today, directors use a variety of editing styles to make
the desired emotional and artistic statement. It is not uncommon to find
variations of invisible and emphatic editing within the confines of one
scene.

Editing Patterns

Besides editing styles, the editor will be concerned about editing patterns. Traditionally, the aesthetics of editing has been based on a variation of patterns. Here are the most important ones:

Spatial forms: At times, the editor tries to achieve pleasing similarities as he cuts from one scene to the next:

Cuts between similar objects. (Christmas tree decorated, and Christmas tree perishing in a trash bin.)
Cuts between objects with similar shape. (Balloon floating through the air, and fat lady eating cake.)
Cuts between similar movements. (Train moving from left to right, ambulance moving from left to right.)
Cuts where the center of emphasis is on the same spot on the screen. (Microscope on screen right, explosion on screen right.)

Plot action: The new shot results out of a previous motive. (Terrorists race through a half destroyed village. People barricade their doors and windows.)
Response cut: Characters respond to each other during dialogue.
Symbolic cuts: Connection in terms of idea or emotion (Wine glasses lined up, a wedding reception.)

Cut-away: A shot taking place at the same time as the main action, but not directly involved with the main action, is called a cut-away. They are often used for overcoming continuity gaps when there is not enough footage for the main action. When properly used, cut-aways will not interfere with the story line.

Insert: The close-up of what an actor sees is called an insert.

Match cut: A cut between shots of the same subject in what appears as a continuous time span is referred to as a *match cut.* The rule is to cut on *motion.* Cutting on motion helps to cover small mismatches from one shot to the other, since it is the *action* that draws the viewer's attention. Action should overlap as much as possible from one shot to the next, to give the editor some space as he matches one movement to the next. If we show a girl in a MEDIUM SHOT as she raises a glass to her lips, and follow the movement in a CLOSE-UP as she drinks, we should film action in the first shot past the point where the action stops, and should begin the CLOSE-UP with part of the action already completed in the MEDIUM SHOT. Extreme care must be taken that everything remains the same during both shots. Facial expression, position of head and body, direction of look—all must remain identical.

Jump cut: Several years ago, every poorly made match cut was called a jump cut. But since the influence of director Jean-Luc Godard, the jump has become accepted. The most commonly used jump cut is achieved by simply cutting out footage that would give the sequence normal continuity. Rapid sequences of jump cuts can have both informational and emotional effect. During jump cuts, information is supplied in isolated bits. This produces an immediate, sharp *focus on the immediate shot.* The relationships between these emphasized bits are established through the pattern developing in the sequence. This pattern of seemingly unrelated cuts is most effective in highly emotional scenes, such as flashbacks and dream sequences.

Editing Equipment

To edit a film, the editor needs some way of cutting, viewing and putting the footage into a new order. He needs:

Viewer
Film rewinds
Splicer
Bin
Cans and reels
Leader

Viewer

The viewer should present a sharp and bright image. Its screen should be sufficient in size so that the image can be easily seen. You should be able to wind film through it fairly quickly and it should be easy to load. A viewer should always be checked for its working condition. Watch out for overheating, and that it works scratch free. Viewers are excellent for quickly arranging shots and searching for footage.

Pacing is more easily judged from the big screen. Most viewers employ a prism for projecting the image onto the viewer's screen, but the image is never as clear as one thrown by a projector. Consequently, focus cannot be decided by using the viewer.

Splicer

You will find four basic types of splices and splicers on the market:

Mylar tape splice: perforated (block splicer)
Mylar tape splice: unperforated (Guillotine)
Cement splice
Cement splice heated (hot splice)

The two main groups, Mylar and Cement, have their advantages and disadvantages, all worth understanding.

Mylar splice: Both ends of the film are butted against each other, and a piece of perforated Mylar tape which is very much like any ordinary type of tape is put across the shot on both sides. No frames are lost when the tape is taken off and another shot is inserted. No part of the film needs to be scraped off. Consequently, we do not see a flash during projection. However, since the splice is thicker than the film, it will throw the image out of focus the moment it moves through the gate. The Mylar splice can be made much faster than a cement splice and requires less skill by the editor. Mylar splicing is therefore the preferred method to cut the workprint.

Guillotine splice: The guillotine splicer uses unperforated Mylar tape. The splicer itself perforates the tape. The skilled editor will work very fast using this splicer. The cost of the individual splice is less than if perforated tape is used, however the rental fee on this splicer is far higher than for the splicer using perforated tape.

Cement splice: Using the cement splice method, the editor must first scrape off a tiny portion of both film ends to be bonded together. A cement splice is made by overlapping the two sections of the film, and joining and dissolving the base of one into the base of the other. The two sections become one, though the film itself becomes thicker at the point of overlap. On projection this splice can be seen as a tiny flash. This flash can be seen much more easily on negative film where it appears white, than on reversal film where it appears as a tiny dark line. However, you will achieve invisible splicing if you use A & B rolls (16mm) for your final answer print.

In conclusion we may say:

Mylar splicing should be used for the workprint because it is easier to handle, the work is done faster, and even a less skilled editor might be able to do a fairly good job. Mylar splicing should definitely be used during production, when dailies have to be assembled. (Mylar splices should be removed by ultrasonic cleaning, the best method of cleaning film.)

Cement splices should be used for your answer print. A cement splice covers less area than the Mylar splice and is thinner than the Mylar. When using a cement splice you will lose a frame every time you wish to change a cut. For sound cutting however, cement splices are inferior to Mylar splices, as they cause drops in the sound level.

Leader: Film leader can be purchased from either your lab, or from the place which provided you with raw stock. The least expensive leader is called lightstruck leader; it is a yellowish-white undeveloped film. Leader is used for *slugging* (the replacement of damaged footage), so you know how much film has been lost, and to mark the *head* (beginning) and *tail* (end) of every roll. Every roll of film should have some identifying marks on both head and tail. A nonwater-based marking pen should be used to write on the leader.

The Workprint

Your assistant editor will have *synced* all dailies in order by the time principal photography is completed. It is now that the editor (in some cases the director himself) and his staff make their appearance. Usually the editor will retain the assistant editor. At times, if speed is of the essence, he will bring in a second assistant editor. Later on he will add a sound effects editor and a music editor. Both of these editors will stay on the job for about four weeks, while the editor and his assistants will work on the picture between two and three months.

First, the editor will have the assistants assemble the dailies into logical sequences (Everything that takes place in the living room will be put together. The same holds true for all scenes that take place on the beach, and on the road, etc.). The editing of a motion picture moves as follows:

1. Rough cut or first assembly.
2. Three quarter cut (the film is smooth and continuous in its appearance, music and sound has been added).
3. Director's cut (the director has the right to change scenes and sequences).
4. Producer's cut (the producer has the right to change scenes and sequences).
5. Final cut (the last cut before the answer print is made).

It is true, a workprint will have to take abuse as it goes first through the picture printing process, and later through the sound editing phases. Still, it is wise to handle your workprint with care. Often it is the workprint that serves as a basis for the demo reels distributors insist upon. While the film is in post-production, the distribution company will take a fifteen to twenty-minute demo reel to Cannes, Milan, or the American Film Market in Los Angeles to get the required pre-sales on your film.

When handling your workprint, do not allow dust, scratches or fingerprints to mar the surface. The editors should make it a habit to wear white gloves. No film should ever be wound so tight as to cause scratch marks. Scratches might also be caused when the film is handled by the lab developer, or most commonly by the projector. Base scratches can usually be buffed. If a scratch appears on the print and not on the negative, you may be able to tell if the scratch is an emulsion scratch. If this is the case, there is little you can do about it.

In case you have to stretch your budget to the limit, and only if you are working with 16mm reversal stock, you may consider making a very rough cut of your original and have that be the workprint. You must have reversal film for this process, since you can judge positive shots more easily than negative shots. If you want to take this road, be certain that you have an expert editor doing the workprint. Once your original has been damaged or scratched, there is nothing you can do. I think it is more sensible to spend the money to have your dailies "workprinted" than to make a rough cut from your original.

Sound

Sound, including music, sound effects and oral statements, can be expressive of emotions. It can, like the visual image on the screen, express symbolism and mood. In any case, sound has its own unique relationship to the visual image on the screen. The motion picture at its best is visual art, and an overreliance on words might easily swamp its visual concept. Still, dialogue is the artistic device to reveal character, to express emotion, and to keep the story line moving ahead. Dialogue is an integral part of any film. At times it can be juxtaposed against the visual image, strengthening this image. Patterns of dialogue may run like a leitmotif throughout the entire picture. In "Juliet of the Spirits," a meaningless dialogue of nothing but words—words—words surrounds Giulietta throughout the film. In "Last Year in Marienbad," the sparseness of vocal expression makes the same artistic statement of emotional emptiness.

After dialogue we can classify sound as:

Natural sound
Sound effects
Music

Natural Sound

Any kind of action is accompanied by some kind of sound. Naturally, we want to hear the sound of a jet plane taking off, we want to hear the door slamming shut, we want to hear the young man whistling a tune, we want to hear the paper crackle as the child opens his birthday gift. But also the reverse is true, a certain noise is distinctive of a certain action. Natural sound often takes over as a source of information when the picture, in terms of time or space, is limited. For instance if we *see* the actress walking towards her dressing room and *hear* thunderous applause, we know she had a tremendous success. However, if we *see* the actress walking to her dressing room, *hear* only sporadic and forced applause, and someone whispering and giggling, we know she has failed. In this respect sound contributes to the story line without taking up time.

Natural sound is a highly effective device to express emotion and mood. In "When a Stranger Calls," the dripping sound of the faucet in the kitchen contributed immensely to the mood of the scene as it personified the female character's increasing fear. The sound of the dripping faucet became louder and more demanding as the scene moved to its climax, the appearance of the intruder.

Distortion of sounds and voices is another effective method of using sound in a symbolic way. A character's emotional state can be suggested by increasing or decreasing the natural sound in his environment to parallel his feelings. Footsteps, the ringing of a telephone, the tapping of a heel against the floor can be raised to hysterical amplification, and may easily become more expressive than the visual image.

Separate sounds can also be used to develop a counterpoint against the visual image. In this respect the filmmaker divorces sound from the image on the screen. In "A Place in the Sun," as we see the judge's gavel being raised, we hear the cry of the loon that was heard when Roberta drowned.

Overlapping sound is one of the basic expressive devices. It is equally effective for:

Marking transitions between fully developed scenes.
Giving information about a time lapse.
Dream sequences and flashback scenes.

Sound in Juxtaposition to Visual Image
Sound expresses the *emotions of the characters*, while the visual image represents the *reality* of the moment. In "The World of Suzy Wong," the lovers have to part. The journalist goes back to England while Suzy remains in Hong Kong. The lovers stand silently facing each other, he avoiding her eyes by busily packing his bags. She, equally tense, avoiding his eyes, hands him shirt after shirt while from far off the music box he gave her at their first meeting plays.

Sound Effects
Sound effects are an integral part of the sound track. Their function is to reveal the reality of the moment to the viewer. Sound effects are usually related to things happening right here and now. We see the car taking off, we hear the screech of the tires on the road, we hear the motor accelerating as the car moves faster, we see the police officer raising his gun, we hear the gunshot.

Music
Background music may either be composed for your picture, or you may buy it "canned" as you would buy your other sound effects. Having music composed may add tremendously to the emotional strength of your film, if you can afford to pay for a first rate composer. (Lalo Schiffrin's scores add to each and every Clint Eastwood picture.) If you intend to have your score written, you may do well to have the composer come on the film together with the director and the director of photography. The score must be composed and it must be recorded. The entire process is time consuming and expensive.

Unless you can afford an experienced composer it is better to rely on pre-recorded (canned) music. Of course, you cannot use any tape or record you feel is right for your film. You'll have to pay a certain amount, usually between $300 to $1000 or even more, for the rights to the music. It is best to rely on the sound lab doing your sound work for your pre-recorded music. Most labs own an extensive library and are very helpful in selecting the right music for your film, and for your budget.

The average movie audience absorbs the background music, hardly ever being aware of it. Yet, background music contributes substantially. When run without underlying music, a film will lose half of its meaning. Background music serves as:

Source of information
Expression of the actor's emotion

Source of information: Burt Bacharach's music actually contributed to the characterization of the leads in "Butch Cassidy and the Sundance Kid," and in "Rebecca," one comes to associate the haunting, frightening melodies with of the former Mrs. De Winter.

Expression of the actor's emotions: The composer has to be careful not to confuse the *actor's emotion* with the *incident on the screen.* An audience might be led astray by musical misinformation, that is, the telegraphing of a soon-to-happen incident. For example, we see a girl walking towards a haunted house. She has to deliver some message from her uncle. It is an ordinary, warm summer evening. The scene would be scored incorrectly if we were to hear an eerie melody. Remember, the score expresses the actor's mood and emotion. The far off cry of any owl, the chirping of crickets would be more in keeping with effective filmmaking. However, as soon as she opens the door and we are shocked by the zoom shot of the one-eyed monster, then, a loud, piercing sound would be appropriate.

Generally speaking, background music has no independent purpose, but services the story.

Sound Editing

Once the sound is recorded it will be sent to a sound lab to be transferred to 35mm *magnetic* film, called MAG. Magnetic film, both 16mm and 35mm, is exactly like camera film, except that oxide replaces the light sensitive emulsion used on camera film. Sound can be either transferred flat or it can be equalized. Often is is necessary to have the sound equalized. When properly equalized, some unwanted background noises may be reduced, and other sound made more intelligible.

As soon as the sound is returned from the sound lab, it is broken down into single rolls that match the picture rolls. It is the sound editor's job to edit sound and picture to the requisite synchronization.

Moviola

The editor will use either a 16mm or 35mm Moviola. The Moviola is the standard editing machine used in the United States. It consists of a motorized viewer placed next to a motorized sound reproducer. The sound head is connected to the picture head. Both can be interlocked so they run together. (The Moviola's sound reproduction system is not up to par, so you should not judge sound quality too severely.)

If the machine is improperly adjusted, the Moviola will tear the perforations on your film.

Synchronizing

The editor either cuts the sound to match the picture, or he plugs the picture for wild sound. For those sections of the film that are without sound he will attach leader to the sound track. As soon as the sound has been properly laid next to the picture, a start mark should be placed on both the picture film and the sound film at corresponding areas of synchronization. The start mark, usually an "X," tells where both line up.

It is beneficial to have the rushes *edge numbered.* Edge numbering machines use several code letters and numbers that are placed on the film at one-foot intervals. You should request your own code. Edge numbering makes editing much easier. The editing time saved is worth the money you have to spend.

Continuity

Continuity applies to the sound as well as to the picture. Both should run in a smooth progression. At times, sound is more continuous than the picture. Imagine, if you will, a busy office scene. We cut from group to group, show the sales manager on the telephone, follow his secretary as she searches for a lost file, catch two pretty girls gossiping, observe the harassed look of the office boy, while everything is pulled together by the continuous sound of typewriters going a hundred miles an hour.

To achieve sound continuity, background levels must match. The sound quality should be the same on either side of the cut. However, slight mistakes can be corrected during the mix. In case background levels do not match, some natural sound, also called *room tone,* may be added. Room tone simply is the background sound of any environment. It is beneficial to record some room sound at every location where you film. Often this natural sound can be used to bridge gaps in dialogue.

The Mix

If you use a synchronized sound track, you need a mix. Basically a mix is a re-recording session. It is a long, involved, nerve wracking and very costly part of your post-production. You should only use the best sound lab you can afford. Five minutes of film may take up to two hours of recording time depending on the complexity of your sound track and the knowledge of the mixer. Most likely you will work with three sound tracks:

Dialogue track
Sound effects track
Music track

These tracks will, at times, operate individually, and at times simultaneously, depending on the sound plot. The mixer adjusts the level for each track and filters them to get the best result. Whenever one sound merges into another there must be at least one foot of overlap. All tracks must be synchronized with each other and with the picture. You should supply the mixer with a cue sheet, informing him at which points each track has sound and at which points he should expect blank leader.

Optical Track
The completed mix sound track is delivered in three forms:

1/4" tape with sync signals recorded on it
35mm or 16mm magnetic film
Optical master track

The optical track will have to be lined up with the cut rolls of the original film before it will be sent out for final printing. Like all low-budget film producers you will probably distribute overseas. In order to sell your picture you'll need a *three-stripe*. One of the stripes, the dialogue stripe will be removed to be replaced with the language of the buying country, while sound and sound effect stripes will remain. It is somewhat more expensive to get a three-stripe, but is a necessity if you wish to make foreign sales.

The Answer Print

The original negative must be conformed to the workprint before an answer print can be struck. This is a difficult, time-consuming and delicate task. Needless to say you need a professional negative cutter to work on your negative. Extreme care must be taken not get dust, fingerprints or scratches on the original. Splices must be well made. A break in the film during printing would be disastrous. Basically, every splice in the workprint will tell the cutter where to cut. However, if you have extended the shot, you should mark the splice by drawing two short parallel lines across the joint. Negative cutters prefer to work by matching edge numbers with the ones printed onto the workprint. For this reason you should make certain that every shot is marked with a latent edge number. You will save the editor's time and your money. Matching pictures by eye is difficult and time consuming.

Your optical sound track must be aligned with the printer roll so that the lab can place it alongside the picture.

Timing the Answer Print
Nowadays, labs use computers to do the color correction on your film. Much footage will be saved this way, as you are able to print "up" (lighter) or "down" (darker). You also will be able to intensify, or diminish any color seen on your one light workprint. It is the responsibility of the cinematographer to supervise this "timing."

Opticals
You'll have to go to a special lab, an "optical house," to get your optical effects done. These effects are very expensive, and you should consider at length whether you really need the optical. The times where every change of scene was indicated by "fades" have long passed. Of course, if you are doing a horror or science fiction film, you will be faced

with a number of necessary opticals. Still, do not let them sneak up on you. Optical and special effects should be indicated in the script and must be an integral part of your budget. The following is a list of some of the most common special effects:

FADE IN: The shot gradually fades in.
FADE OUT: The shot gradually fades out.
DISSOLVE: Two shots are superimposed, and gradually the second shot emerges out of the first one.
WIPE: The second shot pushes the first one off the screen.
CHANGE OF IMAGE: An element in the picture is enlarged.
SKIP FRAMING: Action is speeded up by printing only some of the frames of the original. (Very helpful for car chases).
DOUBLE FRAMING: Action is slowed down by printing each frame twice or more.
MULTIPLE EXPOSURE: Images are superimposed.
FREEZE: Shots can be lengthened by repeating a frame over and over. Freeze is often used while the end titles roll. I would strongly suggest that you forget about using freeze frame at the end of your film, and put the money saved to better use by adding to production values somewhere else.

Let me repeat here, opticals are expensive. They might cost you more than the rest of the budget. Before considering any opticals or special effects, find out whether these could be done directly in final printing.

Titles

You will go to a title house to get your titles made. If you choose "hot press" titles on simple title cards the cost involved won't eat you out of house or home. Yet the cost will be exorbitant if you should choose animation, or any other elaborate effects. Nowadays film titles tend to be fairly simple and on the conservative side. You, the small, low-budget producer should not try to compete with your mega-bucks competitor as far as titles are concerned. Take it easy, save your money.

Some films feature superimposed titles—the titles are superimposed over the action of the film. Granted, this way of titling is very effective, and immediately will give your picture a certain gloss. Still, these titles do require opticals, and you should seriously consider whether the added "glamour" is worth the money.

Final Printing

Once the editing has been completed, the negative will go back to the lab for final printing. At this point you should decide whether all prints, including the release prints, will be made from your original, or whether you will have a duplicate negative—called "dupe"—made. I would strongly recommend to go through the expenses of the dupe. The dupe is cut from an intermediate fine-grain master positive. It is usually less expensive to take release prints from a dupe than from the original negative. As you add one generation there is, of course, some added grain and loss of picture definition. Still, it is a small price to pay to save your negative from excessive handling.

After you receive your answer print or first trial print you evaluate it:

- Has the original been properly cut?
- The print should show no defects, such as scratches. (Check out the source of defects with your lab. If it was their fault they must reprint without charge.)
- Check the timing—Is the color properly balanced? Most likely there are some flaws. Go over these with the timer, and have the lab correct them without charge.

At times it will take a second trial print to have everything corrected to your satisfaction. The first successful print you receive is called the release print.

Fade out ....

The last foot of film has been shot, the gaffer has turned off the arcs, the mixer has packed away the Nagra, the script supervisor has closed her script, the cinematographer has labeled his last can of film—the film is finished.

The last page of this book has been written, this book is finished.

It is a little sad to say "goodbye and good luck" after all the time we spent together. I hope FILM PRODUCING: LOW-BUDGET FILMS THAT SELL has given you the insight and advice you need to make your own successful motion pictures.

Remember everything starts with a dream.

Dreams become goals, goals become actions and actions will turn your dreams into reality. Therefore, do not let others tell you "it cannot be done." Do not let anyone look down on you, or joke about your efforts. By the same token, have the wisdom to recognize and to acknowledge the borders of your expertise, and the humbleness to let others teach you the things you do not know.

Carry the responsibility of being a creator of mass media—a creator of thoughts and ideas that may influence many lives.

Fight for your rights, but respect the rights of others as well.

Be grateful for the creative input of everyone associated with your motion picture.

Most of all, try to help others to get a foothold in this difficult but exciting and gratifying industry of ours, so you may look at your film proudly before you say:

THAT'S A WRAP